The Breathing Organization

Allan,
Thank you for your kindness
and support with the elections
and everything else. You are
a true friend!

ISBN 143480836X | EAN-13 9-781434-808363

10TH ANNIVERSARY EDITION

The Breathing Organization

TECHNIQUES FOR EFFECTIVE LEADERSHIP

FRANK W. BENNETT

To my supportive and loving family.
Thank you for all of your
encouragement over the years.

To all of my friends. I cannot
thank you enough for your support.

TABLE OF CONTENTS

BOOK I: A MEANINGFUL LIFE EXPERIENCE

BOOK II: LEARNING TO BREATHE

ACKNOWLEDGMENTS

First and foremost I would like to recognize my parents, William and Rachel Bennett, who have supported me through all of life's ups and downs. Thank you for all of your support over the years.

I owe much gratitude to Jessica Harden who edited the first edition of the book.

Thank you to Victoria Caldwell who was heavily involved with the creation of this edition including designing the revised front cover. Thank you to Laura Hendrickson for her editing efforts on the new edition.

Lastly, I am dedicating this book to the memory of Boyd Clarke. The primary stock holder in The Tom Peters Company and cofounder of Bluepoint Leadership Development, Boyd was a successful writer and lecturer primarily on leadership issues.

I first spoke to Boyd about a few years back when he responded, by phone, to a letter I sent him praising one of the staff members at The Tom Peters Company. Despite his busy schedule, he stayed on the phone with me for at least half an hour. During this conversation I told him about the book I was writing. After I briefly described the subject matter of the book, he told me that he would be willing to help me in any way I needed and he gave me his cell phone number. Over the next year, we spoke every few months about my progress.

The last time I spoke to Boyd was in late March 2005. I was writing the later chapters of the book, and we discussed a few of the concepts that I was working through.

I finished the initial writing on *The Breathing Organization* on Saturday, June 25, 2005 around 8:30pm. I planned on emailing a complete copy of the book to Boyd at the end of the week after I had done some minor revisions. Unfortunately, I never got to show the final draft to Boyd. On Saturday, the same day that I finished writing the book, Boyd succumbed to cancer and passed away.

I would like to thank Boyd for his contribution to my work. Without his encouragement and advice, I don't think I would have completed this project.

His support and attention gave me hope on difficult days. He made me believe that my work was important. Thank you, Boyd. I will miss you. This book is for you.

INTRODUCTION TO NEW EDITION BY THE AUTHOR

My original goal in writing *The Breathing Organization* was to take common issues I would run into in my consulting practice and discuss them in a book so that a broader audience could benefit.

While my primary goal for writing the book was to teach, I must admit I have gained so much more from the experience. Over the first five years after writing the book I had the opportunity to help hundreds of organizations ranging from large multi-nationals to small start-ups. In a single week in 2007, I consulted for a five person tech start-up in Dallas, conducted a workshop at Microsoft campus in Redmond, Washington, and spoke at University of California at Irvine. These experiences reinforced my already strong conviction that all business is about people. Regardless of the business sector, size of the business, competition, or their financial situation, almost always the organization's current situation is driven by the personality and/or leadership style of one key person. In healthy organizations key people are the driving strength of the organization, in unhealthy situations they serve as toxins. I am constantly amazed at how even in organizations with thousands of employees this ends up being true.

In 2011, I closed my consulting practice to become the CEO of The National Quilt Museum in Paducah, Kentucky. The museum is a global destination art museum that promotes quilt and fiber art. At this time, I also moved from Dallas to Paducah. Paducah is a wonderful community made up of about 25,000 hard working people. As with many communities of this size, a large percentage of the population works at a handful of large companies. Having now been in this community for five years, I have gained appreciation for the total impact that bad leadership can have on organizations. As I write these words, one employee change at one of our most public companies is creating a strain on the entire community.

A multi-national corporation has a location in the area. It is one of the area's largest employers. About a year ago the company brought in a general manager that has demonstrated by his words and actions that he thinks he is smarter than everyone that would choose to live in this area and has no interest in outside opinions. Over the time he has been here the culture at the organization he runs has gone from fun and healthy to fear driven.

As an example, about six months ago the company's national parent organization asked employees around the country to take a survey on their overall job satisfaction. The survey scores at the local branch run by this terrible manager were some of the worst in the country as most employees are very unhappy (this is just the ones that have stayed, turnover has been very high since the new manager took over). After the survey results were distributed to local management, employees were asked to come to a meeting to discuss the issues. Not a single employee would discuss what they were unhappy about for fear they would be fired or punished in some way by this manager. They all sat there stone faced. In addition to the staff issues, this manager has made a number of poor decisions that have led to hundreds of customers deciding they will no longer be back.

My point in telling this story has nothing to do with revenue or profits, but rather, on the impact to the entire community that this one bad leader is having. In the time he has been at the helm employee turnover has skyrocketed, average employee paycheck has decreased since tips are down as the number of visitors has reduced and morale is so low you can actually feel it when you walk into the facility. People that pay their bills and take care of their families by working at this business are struggling to make smaller paychecks stretch. If they have left the business they are having to travel further or work more difficult hours at other companies to make ends meet. In addition, their disposable income has reduced impacting every business in the community.

Suffocation management doesn't just have an impact on profits and losses; it has an impact on people's lives. Ten years ago if you had asked me why I wrote this book I would have said that I wanted to improve companies. Now if you ask me the same question I will say that I want to impact lives. This is what I've gained most from writing the book.

I hope you enjoy the book and implement the tools discussed. If you are a key leader at an organization remember that your job is more important than your paycheck. You have a responsibility that goes way past your own paycheck. Your actions impact the lives of your employees, their families, your patrons, your vendors, and the entire community that your organization serves.

INTRODUCTION

"Breathe. Let go. And remind yourself that this very moment is the only one you know you have for sure."

—Oprah Winfrey

Without water we can live for days, without food we can live for weeks, but without oxygen we can only live for minutes. In a sense oxygen is the breath of life. It is a vital nutrient in our bodies. It is essential for the health of our brain, nerves, glands, and internal organs. Our need for it is constant and immediate.

Many debilitating psychological and physical health problems can be linked to limited, quick, and/or short breathing. Short, poor breathing contributes to depression, stress, mental sluggishness, lack of energy, irritability, nervousness, and reduced productivity. Extended short or poor breathing can lead to vision impairment, hearing loss, organ degradation, heart problems including heart attacks, strokes, and cancer.

When we can't breathe all other bodily functions become totally unimportant. When stress levels go up breathing quickens and becomes shallower. Less oxygen goes to the brain. Brain functioning decreases along with a decrease in energy, creativity, and productivity. Our brains run out of gas. Simply stated, when our breathing is limited, all other human output degrades. We simply shut down.

Conversely, those of us who achieve high quality breathing live the healthiest lives. Research has shown that people whose breathing is deeper and calmer experience less stress, slower aging, fewer health problems, more creativity, more energy, more productivity, and a generally more positive outlook on the world.

Try the following experiment. Take a few deep breaths doing the following: inhale through the nose and hold it in for two seconds and then exhale through the nose slowly. Do this three times and see if you don't become calmer and more comfortable. Now picture yourself sitting at the desk at your office. You are engaging in your daily job tasks. Did your breathing become more shallow and quick? The stresses around you in your work world cause this to occur. Just thinking about your job and the stresses involved limit your breathing. This same cycle happens to millions of people every day who work in what I will call "suffocating organizational culture." When your breathing became shallower and quick your ability to be creative, multitask, focus on tasks, and your overall mental functions diminished. The amount and quality of work you are able to produce as well as your overall satisfaction with your job greatly diminish. Multiply this phenomenon by the total number of people in your organization and you have an entire culture operating at a fraction of their potential.

The word *organizations* share the same root word as *organisms* for a reason. They achieve better results when they are able to breathe. Like humans, organizational effectiveness is degraded by practices that limit breathing. As humans, we have a roadmap to effective health. We know universally that actions such as eating quality foods, getting regular exercise, quality sleep, and meditation increase our health. Organizations also have a roadmap to good health. There is a set of core perceptions that managers at all levels must champion in order for the organization to breathe.

When an organization stops living by these core understandings it becomes unhealthy. If these core understandings are not addressed quickly, these stresses lead to organizational disease. Regardless of internal initiatives, strategies, business plans, mission statements, or talent, the organization will suffocate if it does not put these core understandings at the foreground of all management practices.

The degradations that occur in organizations are given names such as reduced profits, employee turnover, employee apathy, unsatisfied clientele, and disengagement. The ultimate result of the negligence within an organization is almost exactly the same as that of a poorly treated human body. The organization becomes increasingly sick as time goes by.

The Breathing Organization will serve as a roadmap toward better organizational health. As proper diet and exercise are at the core of a healthy lifestyle, the concepts discussed in this book are at the core of a healthy organization. By implementing these understandings and working to maintain them you will achieve a level of success beyond what you currently consider possible and maintain this success for decades to come.

"To achieve long term business success you must create a meaningful life experience for clients, employees, and owners."

—Frank Bennett

BOOK I

A MEANINGFUL
LIFE EXPERIENCE

CHAPTER 1

"I understand"

"I understand... but"

"I am sorry about that... "

Bill sits at his desk back peddling while an AceCalc client gives a never ending monologue describing all of the reasons why he has decided, after fifteen years, to start using a competitor.

"I am sorry that you're upset, let me come out personally and work through some of these issues with you", Bill states quickly between the clients rants.

"Don't bother!" the client replies emphatically, "We just don't know who you guys are anymore. You aren't the same company your uncle created."

Bill leans back in his desk, throws his phone headset on to his computer keyboard and takes a deep breath. The client that AceCalc just lost had been with them for over 18 years and accounted for six percent of the company's gross revenue during the previous year. For most CEO's, losing a client worth this much to their company would be a primary concern, but in Bill's world, this is just another drop in the bucket.

The company for which Bill finds himself at the helm is fraught with problems and sinking fast. In addition to losing a key client, earlier today, AceCalc lost one of its vice presidents and founding employees. "Out of nowhere," at least according to the way Bill saw it, this Vice President chose to go work for a competitor. He told Bill that he had been miserable in his job for about two years. "I feel like my talents are going to waste here," the VP said with visible anguish as he spoke.

Bill tried to fix the problem by offering the VP more money if he would stay.

"I don't want more money. The job I am taking pays about half of what I earn here," the VP responded, "I just don't feel at home here anymore."

After about half an hour of sitting in despair, wondering what to do next, Bill decides to take a look at the financial books. He pulls the company records from twelve months before he became CEO. A year and a half ago, when Bill took over the company, AceCalc was producing steady growth due mostly to a mix of long term client relationships and steady employee performance. The year before Bill became CEO, the company recorded a 92% employee retention level. Over the past twelve months, Bill has seen that number drop to 43%. Productivity has dropped in every department within this 200 person company. The inside and outside sales departments are seeing drastically lower results. The order processing and delivery departments are making more mistakes than ever before and employees are taking three times as many sick days.

Over the previous ten years the company had consistently seen 10-30% growth per year. This year, however, AceCalc has seen negative growth for the first time in a decade. This is the result of both decreasing sales and poor client retention. Historically, AceCalc prided themselves on the quality and longevity of their client relationships. On one of the walls in the executive office a sign reads, "80% of the clients who came along in year one are still with us". The information on this sign became false last year when several of these clients jumped ship. As a result of the company's downward turn, for the first time in the companies 25 year history the board of directors recommended layoffs.

Bill is a 48 year old man who has spent his entire adult life in 'Corporate America'. He started his career with a mid-sized manufacturing company in Wisconsin. During his first experience in the corporate world, Bill got a crash course in the politics of the boardroom. He learned how to take care of his own interests and maintain control over his surroundings. He learned who the players were and how the game was played. He learned that the key to climbing the corporate latter was making yourself look better than all of the other employees in the eyes of upper management. He had become very good at playing the political game and received several promotions. Unfortunately, after 22 years he found himself without a job when the executive office politics that led to his success swung against him. When it was all said and done, he left this job with some resume' experience, a generic reference letter from the CEO, sixty pounds of extra weight around his stomach, and high cholesterol.

After a few months of interviewing, Bill landed his first Vice Presidential position for a national distribution company based in Texas. He thought he would spend the rest of his adult life with the company. Unfortunately, they were bought by a competitor and Bill was laid off. All of the employees at this company were pressured into working a minimum of 70 hours per week. Bill was no exception; he lived in his office. During his time in Texas his eleven year marriage ended.

According to Bill, "She did not understand how important my job was to me."

Three and a half years ago Bill brought his history of corporate experience to AceCalc. AceCalc was founded by Bill's uncle, Jack Free, who had been trying to convince Bill to come aboard for many years. Bill had many reservations about working for AceCalc. In his mind he would be taking a significant demotion. Bill considered himself to be way over qualified for the Vice Presidential job that Mr. Free was offering him. He thought of himself as a very big fish going into a small, and in many ways, insignificant pond. Despite reservations, Bill took the job mostly because he had not received any other interesting offers at the time. Although he never expressed it, he did not think he would be with the company very long.

Bill had worked as Vice President of Marketing for about a year and a half when tragedy occurred. Mr. Free was driving to work on an ordinary Tuesday when a drunk driver hit his car killing both himself and Mr. Free. After the accident AceCalc was in disarray. Mr. Free had planned to work for several more years, and as such, had never discussed the company succession plan with anyone. After his passing, company leaders received a call from Mr. Free's personal attorney. In an addendum to his will, Mr. Free stated that he wished for the company to always be run by a member of his family. He recommended that Bill become the CEO. Bill becoming CEO would create a little friction within the company leadership. Bill had only been with the company for a few years and he would be skipping over several more experienced VP's. The company board of directors could technically have overruled Mr. Free's wishes but chose not too out of respect.

On his first day as CEO, Bill gave a speech to the entire staff. In this speech he talked about his admiration for his uncle's legacy and the honor he felt in being entrusted with its stewardship. He spoke of how important he considered all of the employees to be and how much he appreciated all of their contributions. Finally, to much applause he stated, "I intend to follow in Mr. Free's footsteps... I intend to keep things the same as they have always been so that we can continue to grow as we always have."

....

Frustrated and highly stressed, Bill tells his receptionist to hold all of his calls for the remainder of the day, and then leaves the office. He decides to take a walk in a local park.

He thinks about his job...

He thinks about his family...

He thinks about his place in the world... After slowly walking several laps around the park, Bill sits down on a bench at least a quarter mile away from anyone. His head spinning; he wonders how everything could have gone so wrong so quickly. He mutters under his breath, "What could I have done differently... I kept all of the policies and procedures exactly as they were under my uncle." Bill feels alone and helpless. He wants to crawl into a corner and hide from the world. After much anguish he falls to his knees and starts to cry.

After spending about an hour in the park, Bill slowly picks himself up and heads for home. At home, he begins rummaging through the boxes in his closet. After about twenty minutes thumbing through old pictures and other mementos, he runs across his AceCalc training notes from three and a half years ago. A brief smile comes over his face as he opens to the first page and sees the letter from Mr. Free welcoming new employees to the company. After a few minutes of flipping through page after page of notes from his first few days at AceCalc, Bill comes up with an idea. He thinks that these notes might be his key to figuring out what has changed since he took over the company. He sits down at his kitchen table and begins to go through item after item looking for a smoking gun. As he reads the memories start flowing back. He sits back and starts to daydream...

CHAPTER 2: TRAINING DAY ONE

Bill reminisces all the way back to his first day with AceCalc. He had been through several executive training classes with previous companies, and he did not expect this one to be much different. With an arrogant swagger, Bill walked into the building for the first time, walked right past the receptionist without a hint of acknowledgment and headed directly to Mr. Free's office. He finds Mr. Free making small talk with his assistant toward the front of his office. After a minute of chatting, Bill asked, "So where is my office?"

Mr. Free responded, "Your office isn't ready yet, but it really doesn't matter. It will be days before you need to use it."

Bill was a little taken aback; he assumed that with his past experience he would only have to go through a cursory training program before starting his job.

Mr. Free began to describe the training process while the two walked down a hall toward the front of the building.

"Before you do anything in your new role as Vice President of Marketing you will spend three days observing how our company does business. In these three days you will talk with people in almost every department. These team members will teach you the basics of how we do business. All you need right now is a pen, a notebook, and this itinerary."

Mr. Free handed Bill an itinerary which included a list of departments he was to observe and when he was to visit each department. At the top of the itinerary was a quotation from Mr. Free:

"Welcome to the AceCalc family. You can sum our entire business up in three words, Meaningful Life Experience. Over the next three days it is your responsibility to gain an understanding of what these three words mean. At the end of your three day training I will personally ask you what you have learned. Good Luck!"

Bill rolled his eyes after reading the introduction. It seemed like another silly mission statement that would be discussed once and then thrown into a drawer. In Bill's experience with previous employers there was a 180-degree difference between the mission statement and the actual way the company did business.

After looking through the departments listed on his itinerary and the titles of the employees he was to "check in" with, Bill was even more confused than before. He was expecting to spend a few days breaking the ice and building a rapport with other executives. Instead, he was to report to some manager in charge of local deliveries in thirty minutes. No company had ever made Bill meet low-end employees as part of a training process to become an executive. Bill thought this seems like a waste of time: these people's jobs have nothing to do with the job duties I will perform as a vice president. Feeling a little annoyed, Bill decided to go along with the training schedule mostly because he did not want to make waves on his first day. As they separated at the end of the hall, Bill turned to Mr. Free and asked him where the delivery department is located.

"Go to the front desk and ask the receptionist: her name is Stacy, she knows the lay of the land around here very well," Mr. Free replied with a smile.

At ten minutes till 9:00am Bill sat down outside the office of the local delivery department manager, Ms. Happy. Still annoyed that he had to go through all of these training rituals, Bill doodled on the three pieces of paper that he had grabbed from a printer in the hall. Although Bill had been told that he would take lots of notes and needed plenty of paper, he did not see the point. After all, he was sure that he knew all of this stuff already.

After a few minutes he heard the loud speaker system come on. It is Mr. Free doing his morning announcements:

"Good Morning everyone, I had nine submissions for yesterday's *Hero of the Day*, which is very exciting. The winner is Bethany Riley in Accounts Receivable. Bethany handled a major problem with grace and class and created a memorable life experience for a client who had previously been a little difficult to deal with. The Ronchester Group was disputing over $4200.00 of invoices and avoiding our phone calls. We were starting to think that we were going to have to take a loss on this money, most of which is over 60 days delinquent. After sending several letters, Bethany took it upon herself to act on the company's "like a friend" principle. Instead of taking aggressive action, she decided to stop by Ronchester Group and get to the bottom of the issue. After waiting for 45 minutes, the head of Accounts Payable for Ronchester agreed to see Bethany. According to Bethany, "It was obvious that Marge was very

frustrated with our company. We had dropped the ball both in regards to our basic client experience practices as well as our "client intimacy" efforts." After venting her frustrations for ten minutes about the poor service she had received, Marge sat back in her chair with her arms crossed waiting for a battle.

Bethany took the stack of invoices that were sitting on the table between the two of them, balled them up, and threw them into the trashcan. "I was trying to break the tension and rebuild the relationship", Marge explained when we talked this morning. Bethany then convinced Marge to get away from the office and join her for coffee at a local shop. "We sat there for an hour talking about kids and movies and just everything," Bethany said. At the end of the coffee break Marge agreed to come back to AceCalc with Bethany, "I wanted her to get to know us at a human level," Bethany gave her the grand tour. She had never been to our offices. Marge loved the attention. As an accounts payable employee at Ronchester she was treated like another pawn in the system. She was used to people just going over her head when they had a problem with her department. This was the first time anyone had taken the time to get to know what is important to her both in her job and in her life. Bethany drove Marge back to Ronchester and intending to simply drop her off and deal with the invoices later. Instead, Marge insisted, "Let's go upstairs and work out all these bills; I want to get our relationship up to date."

Before doing the announcements this morning
I had a chance to speak with Bethany about this
interaction with Ronchester. During the conversation
she gave me a great tip. "Having worked in
Accounts Receivable for two years I have found that
receivables issues are 90% relationship and 10%
money." Congratulation to Bethany for exemplifying
the AceCalc way of doing business. Please extend
your appreciation to Bethany as you see her today.

In other news, I just got word that Bridget O'Connell
in Accounting gave birth to a 7 pound 2 ounce
baby boy at 4:45am. She will be in the office on
Thursday to visit and she will be back to work
next month. That's all I have for now. Everyone
have a great day. I can't wait to hear about today's
meaningful life experiences."

Despite his earlier doubts, Bill found himself jotting down several notes about Mr. Free's announcements. As he was writing Ms. Happy came out to greet him. Ms. Happy was a short woman dressed very conservatively, she spoke quickly and was always in motion. After quickly shaking Bill's hand, she motioned for him to follow her to the loading docks. Before Bill could get a word out Ms. Happy told him that he was going to ride along with one of the drivers so he could observe how they interact with clients. "We have to hurry or we will miss Dwayne, the driver I want you to ride along with," Ms. Happy stated as they hurried to the back of the building. Once again Bill was surprised. He did not think he would be doing grunt work like going on deliveries with "low end" employees, and furthermore he did not see what he could possibly gain from watching front end employees do their jobs.

"Dwayne! Hold up!" Ms. Happy bellowed. A tall gentleman in his mid-thirties turned and smiled at us while we dashed toward him. As they reached Dwayne he calmly offered his hand and introduced himself to Bill. After a few more minutes of loading the truck, Bill hesitantly stepped up into the truck's passenger seat as Dwayne started the van and they took off toward the first stop.

Bill struggled to make small talk still wondering why he was sitting in a delivery van with an employee who was several levels under Bill in the company hierarchy.

"How long have you been with the company," Bill asked?

"Eight years," Dwayne replied.

"Eight years! Bill replied, wondering what had caused this driver to be stuck in this low-end job for so long.

Dwayne explained that he had been offered several promotions over the years but he wasn't really interested. "I have three kids and my wife works sixty hours a week, AceCalc has given me the perfect job for my life priorities. I spend my days delivering products to friends all over the city and I spend afternoons and evenings with my family," Dwayne explained.

This was the second time that Bill had heard an employee refer to a client as a friend. "Why does everyone at AceCalc refer to clients as friends?" Bill asked.

"We have a concept called the 'like a friend principle'. You probably heard Mr. Free refer to it this morning. I could explain it to you, but you will not understand until you see it in action. Let's see some friends and then we'll discuss your question further," Dwayne replied.

Just as Dwayne finished his sentence, they pulled up to a company called Davis Central Customs, Inc. Dwayne drove around to the back of the building where two Davis employees where waiting. As soon as Dwayne saw the employees, a smile came over his face. He pulled the truck up to the loading dock and jumped out. Expecting the usual signing of forms and counting of items in the shipment, Bill tossed his pen and paper onto the dash and walked around the truck to do the courtesy introductions. As he approached the three men, he overheard a conversation about a softball game that had apparently occurred the previous Saturday. After listening for a few minutes, Bill learned that Dwayne and the two Davis employees were part of a softball league that seemed to have some kind of connection to AceCalc. After a few more minutes of small talk, that seemed more like a family reunion then a business transaction, Dwayne said goodbye, and they headed for the next delivery.

Back in the delivery van, Bill asked Dwayne about the discussion he had overheard. "So you and those Davis employees know each other outside of work?" Bill inquired.

"No, not any more than any other client you will meet," Dwayne replied.

"I don't understand."

"AceCalc has a softball league that plays on the fields behind our building. We have twelve teams each made up of half AceCalc employees and half clients. One of The Davis employees that you just met is the shortstop on my team."

Dwayne went on to explain that AceCalc had developed sports leagues for basketball, softball, and volleyball and that each of the leagues was a mix of employees and clients.

"By the way," Dwayne continued, *"You just saw an example of one of the core concepts that we use to build a meaningful life experience for our clients. We acquired Davis as a client six years ago when they became frustrated with one of our competitors. Davis is a company that runs a very tight inventory. Often when we bring them their order, they are down to one or two in stock on many items. It is critical to their business that the order comes before 10:00am each day. I always make them my first delivery. You see, we directly match our offerings to client needs. We know what's important to each client, and we know what's not important. Having an intimate understanding of both 'what is' and 'what is not' important is critical to our business success. This way we are able to provide great service and, at the same time, maximize the use of our resources. Davis fired the company that they used prior to us because their delivery times were inconsistent. As I said, Davis is a company whose chief concern is time. Each of our clients has unique needs, and we make sure that our services match their needs. As Mr. Free often says, "Giving a client the wrong help is like trying to date a millionaire by convincing her that you will be a good provider. No one's needs are met when we do not properly match our offerings to each client's needs. Take Davis, for example, if I didn't know the importance of time to their business, I wouldn't do their delivery until much later in the day. Davis is geographically out of my way."*

A few minutes later they arrived at the second delivery destination. They got out of the van, and Dwayne began loading boxes onto a delivery dolly. Bill followed him through the building to a second floor office. From the looks of the office several people worked there, although no one was at their desk. Bill dropped the boxes in a corner and stopped to get some water. Thinking it was time to go back to the van for the next delivery Bill turned and headed for the door.

"Hang on," Dwayne proclaimed, "We're not done here yet. Would you stop by your best friend's office without saying hello? Dwayne asked in a calm teaching tone. We're going to wait until Stacy comes back; I know she is here because her coffee is still steaming."

After about ten minutes a tall thin women in her fifties walked into the room and smiled at Dwayne. "Hi, Dwayne, are you waiting for me?" she asked.

"Stacy, how is your mother doing," Dwayne asked.

"She's getting better. She should be out of the hospital in a few days; they are just keeping her for observation at this point. Thanks for asking," Stacy replied.

Dwayne continued, "How was the new product meeting last week?"

"Well, the prototypes were good, but they still need some work. It was a fun meeting though. I learned a lot," Stacy replied.

Back in the van, Bill asked Dwayne about the interaction that had taken place between him and the client. "Why did we have to wait for Stacy; don't you see her everyday?" Bill inquired.

"Yea, but one of the principles AceCalc lives by is called 'The Golden Touch'." One of the biggest keys to creating a meaningful life experience is the depth and quality of the personal relationships between employees and clients. The Golden Touch" principle states that each opportunity to touch a client is precious and should be treated like gold. If I had left her office without taking a few minutes to talk, I would have lost a chance to touch a client." "Hey," Dwayne continued, "If I were you I would write that down". Bill was a little taken back at the way Dwayne cavalierly told him to write down what he was saying. After all, Bill thought, "Doesn't he know that I am training to be a Vice President?" After writing a flurry of notes Bill commented, "I am starting to understand what you mean by a meaningful life experience and treating clients as you would treat a close friend, but why did you ask her about some new product meeting at her office last week?"

"It wasn't at her office; it was at our office," Dwayne replied, "She attended one of our new product meetings. She sits on the new product steering team."

Bill really did not understand. First of all, why would AceCalc want a client to be a member of an AceCalc internal committee? Wouldn't this expose our flaws to the outside world? Second, why would a client volunteer to do such a thing? "Is this out of the ordinary, having a client on an internal team?" Bill asked.

"Of course not," Dwayne replied as if the question was silly, "Clients are on every team in the company. This is something else you may want to write down," Dwayne continued, "It's called the 'Law of Connection'.

"I mentioned the importance of every touch earlier; this is a little different. 'The Golden Touch' and 'like a friend' principles are used to build relationships between individuals. We also think that it is important to always be building a relationship between the client and AceCalc as a whole. The more clients know about who we are and what we are about, the more they will trust us and feel like they are a part of our community. Many companies, whether intentionally or unintentionally, build walls between themselves and their clients. We do the opposite; we see all separation as a hindrance to creating a meaningful experience. The 'Law

of Connections' states that we do everything possible to get everyone involved in the company in as many ways as possible. Mr. Free once said that the two greatest keys to building a meaningful life experience for clients are communication and caring. We believe that 95% of lost clients leave a company because of either poor communication or lack of caring. Poor communication leads to assumptions, which are never good for any relationship business or otherwise. Lack of caring leads to alienation, which is almost impossible to overcome."

The van was quiet for several minutes while Bill took in everything he had seen and heard so far. He had only been observing for a few hours, and it had become very clear that this company did things differently than any other company for which he had previously worked.

Dwayne pulled the van up to another company for the third delivery. This seemed to be a small company located in a professional centre near the middle of town. At this point, Bill was excited to meet the client. This was an entirely new experience for him. He was excited about work for the first time in years.

After dropping off fifteen boxes of product in a storage room, they knocked on the door of the company president. The gentleman's name was Hiram Bell. He was a gentleman with a calm demeanor and a warm smile. Seeing Bill and Dwayne at the door, he got up from his desk, and they shook hands.

"How was Vegas?" Dwayne asked.

"It was great; my wife and I caught several shows including Neil Diamond," Hiram responded with a warm smile.

"Are we on for golf on Friday afternoon?" Dwayne asked.

"Sure, I have us scheduled for a tee time at 2:00pm. By the way, tell Robert thanks for helping me with my car, it's running great now," Hiram continued.

After a few more minutes of conversation Bill and Dwayne said goodbye and headed back to the van. Bill was a little confused about a few of the items Dwayne and the client had discussed. At this point Bill was becoming used to seeing things at AceCalc that he had never seen before.

"Are you off on Friday?" Bill asked Dwayne.

"No, why do you ask?" Dwayne replied." "You're playing golf with Mr. Bell?" "That's right," Dwayne replied, not understanding Bill's question.

"How can you play golf with Mr. Bell if you don't have the day off?"

"Its part of my job, Bill. Hiram likes to play golf, and I have the opportunity to continue building a meaningful life experience for my client by playing golf with him"

"But you are a delivery driver?" Bill replied before realizing the harshness of his statement.

"Yeah, but as long as I am creating a meaningful life experience for my clients I am doing my job. I can do anything I need to do to build or maintain a meaningful life experience. After all, my job is not delivering packages; my job is building meaningful life experiences. It just so happens that my specific task is delivering packages."

Bill jotted down some more notes while changing to a new line of questioning. "So you sent one of your friends over to fix Mr. Bell's car?"

"Not quite... I sent out an all-employee email asking if anyone knew how to fix the problem that Hiram was having with his car, and Robert Champion answered the email."

"I think I get it," Bill responded, "Robert helped you build the relationship with Mr. Bell. That was very nice of him, but what did you have to give him for him to agree to do that?" Bill asked sarcastically.

"Nothing, that's part of his job. As far as he's concerned, he was fixing a friend's car. You see, everyone in the company observes the 'like your friend' principle. We don't just treat the customers we touch the most as friends; we treat all clients this way. We see each client as a friend of the entire organization."

"Oh, okay, who is Robert Champion?" Bill asked.

"He is the Vice President of Operations," Dwayne replied.

"The Vice President of Operations!" Bill exclaimed.

This story really hit home for Bill. He had learned a lot about the unique way that AceCalc does business, but in his wildest perceptions he could not see a Vice President helping a relatively small client with a car repair based on a request that was made by a low end employee. At this point, Bill's head was spinning. Not only was this unlike anything he had ever seen, but he couldn't conceive of this concept at all.

....

After the delivery to Hiram Bell's company, Dwayne drove Bill back to AceCalc. Bill was to get together with Ms. Happy for a discussion about what he had witnessed in the field. Bill spent a few minutes going through his notes while waiting for Ms. Happy to finish a meeting.

Suddenly, Ms. Happy burst out of her office and, with a giant smile, she asked Bill how his day had gone. Bill hesitated for a second, thinking back on the whirlwind of experiences and new ideas that made up the first half of his day. Seeming surprised even as the words left his mouth, Bill uttered, "This is different then anything I've ever seen."

Sitting in Ms. Happy's office with the facial expression of a country boy walking in New York City for the first time, Bill seemed almost discombobulated. He was trying to absorb so many new concepts that flew in the face of his 25 years of business experience. His facial expression showed the vulnerability that he felt in admitting to Ms. Happy, a person who would be below him in the company hierarchy that he was completely amazed with what he had seen thus far.

Ms. Happy smiled comfortingly and said, "It's alright. Everyone learns a lot of new things during their first week here, especially those people with years of experience in more traditionally managed businesses."

"So what questions do you have so far Bill," Ms. Happy asked.

"I'm not sure where to start; there's so much new information to absorb," Bill replied while he shuffled through his notes.

"Just give me the top few for now; after all, it's only your first day of training," Ms. Happy replied with a smile and a light chuckle that made him think she had had this very discussion many times in the past.

Bill flipped through his mess of notes for a moment before Ms. Happy stepped in, "I'll tell you what Bill. I'll start the discussion by going over some of the philosophies behind the client practices that you witnessed."

"Today you got to witness what we do in this department; now you need to understand a little more about why we do things this way."

Just as Ms. Happy started to lean back in her chair to begin a bit of a monologue, Bill jumped in and asked if he could borrow some paper before she got started. "I don't want to miss this," Bill proclaimed. After pulling a few pieces of paper from her printer she began.

"At AceCalc we feel that there is a pyramid of customer success. At the bottom of the pyramid is mere customer service. In my experience, companies who focus on customer service tend to do everything right and, at the same time, do nothing great. They smile at clients, are very respectful, say thank you, sometimes even call a person by their name during interactions. These companies make little or no real connection with clients.

"The first level of customer success that we are concerned with is the client experience. With the ever increasing competition in our industry, clients can go anywhere to get the products that we offer. We have to give clients a reason to use our company.

"There are three keys to our client experience. First, a clients experience must be memorable. You can't get clients excited about your offerings if they have no reason to remember you. Second, we are unique. Our client experience is basically a service brand. People should be able to recognize us by the way we do every part of our business. Third, the

experience has to mean something to OUR clients. I think this is the most important key to the client experience. I really like something Mr. Free said once, 'Here at AceCalc we're not trying to be everything to everyone; we're trying to be something life-altering to a core group of people'. Many companies make their offerings bland because they don't want to exclude any potential clients. It's almost like they're trying not to offend anyone. We believe that this is the wrong way to do business. As Mr. Free stated, we are striving to be something very special and exciting to a core group of clients. Everything about us is distinct and bold.

"As you have heard, we are creating a meaningful life experience for our clients. Bland and boring is the opposite of this effort. In my opinion, bland and boring is the enemy of business success."

"But aren't you guys going to push away a lot of potential clients." Bill interjected.

"Yeah, sure, but we don't care. We don't want every client; we want the right clients!" Ms. Happy boldly asserted.

Just as Ms. Happy was getting into the second part of her lecture on client success, a knock came at the door. A tall, thin gentleman named Stephen walked through the door with excitement dripping off of his face.

"I want to turn in a story for hero of the day," Stephen stated.

"Bonnie Kyle in receiving has really gone out of her way today, and she deserves to be nominated." Before he could go into the story, Ms. Happy interrupted, "Stephen that is absolutely wonderful. I want to hear the story, but Bill and I are right in the middle of a discussion. Go ahead and submit it in Mr. Free's office and come back and see me in about half an hour."

After drinking some water and making a comment about Stephen's enthusiasm and team spirit, Ms. Happy went right back to her lecture on clients. It was overtly obvious that this was one of her favorite subjects to discuss.

"So, we talked about the client experience; now let's talk about what makes AceCalc who we are. The highest step in the client success pyramid is 'Client Intimacy'. This is the key to creating a clients meaningful life experience for our clients. You asked me about treating our clients as we would treat our best friend, so you probably have learned about 'The Golden Touch' and the 'Law of Connection.'"

Bill nodded.

"All of these principles are the manifestation of our belief that the key to long- term client relationships is client intimacy. In a nutshell, we believe that the closer our relationship with a client, the more likely they are to stay with us over time. If clients see us as a central part of, not just their business, but also as a central part of their lives, then we have achieved our goal. We want to be part of client's lives in the same way that you would be part of your best friend's life. We do not believe there should be any separation between someone's business life and their personal life. In my opinion, the single greatest key to building a meaningful life experience is intimacy. This is what it is all about."

"So, what if a client doesn't want you to be that closely involved?" Bill inquired.

"That's fine. If that issue comes up, which it does a few times a year, we help the client find a company whose culture and offerings better match their needs. Once again, we don't want every client; we want the right ones. If a client doesn't fit our culture, stringing them along is ultimately an exercise in futility." "By the way," Ms. Happy continued, "Did Dwayne tell you about the client contract?"

Bill looked at her with confusion and said, "Client contract?"

"While doing the deliveries today, did Dwayne talk to any of the clients about AceCalc meetings or board involvement?" Ms. Happy asked.

"Yes, several times," Bill replied, "He told me that every client is on some kind of AceCalc team. I'm glad you brought this up. How do you get all of these clients to serve on these company teams?"

"One of the keys to building a meaningful life experience for clients is involvement. For us to achieve our goals, it is critical that clients are intimately involved with AceCalc in every way possible. Each of our clients has signed a contract outlining their responsibilities as our client."

Bill was so baffled that he did not know what to say. Why in the world would a company put involvement demands on their clients? "Doesn't this turn a lot of clients away?" Bill asked.

"I know this seems counter-intuitive based on your past experiences, but actually the opposite is true. Clients, as well as every human being, want to be a part of something special. The clients who are excited about our company are always looking for ways to become more involved. When you successfully create a meaningful life experience for a client they will become a fanatic for our company. As you work for AceCalc, you will see clients with AceCalc license plates, AceCalc shirts, AceCalc lapel pins, believe it or not, there is even an AceCalc Visa card. We want our clients to be as excited about their association with AceCalc as they are about their favorite sports team. The client contract is part of our overall effort to indoctrinate clients into the AceCalc culture."

While Bill was thinking through what he had just been told, Ms. Happy looked at her watch and realized that she needed to run. "Bill, you will learn much more about our culture and philosophies, tomorrow. I'm sure you have taken in a lot of information today. Go ahead and go through days two and three of your training, and if you still have client questions, feel free to come back and see me. For now, I have to run to a meeting. Tomorrow, you will learn about creating a meaningful experience for employees. It was great spending time with you, Bill. Have a great second day of training." With that Ms. Happy led Bill to the door and dashed off.

Bill got home about an hour later. On his way home, Bill stopped at a local store to pick up a notebook for the next two days of training. After grabbing some dinner, Bill began reviewing his notes. After about an hour and a half of work, he had reduced his notes down to a few key points. He took out a piece of paper, jotted down the key points, and pinned them to a bulletin board in his kitchen.

Keys to Creating Meaningful Life Experience for Clients

1. **Match Offerings to Client Needs**: It builds value and increased increases company efficiency.

2. **Law of Connection**: Continuous communication. We can never over communicate with a client. Take every opportunity to show them that we care. A disconnected or alienated client is as good as gone.

3. **The Golden Touch**: Treat all opportunities to interact with a client as gold. Never take an interaction for granted, or let an interaction be less then meaningful.

4. **Like a Friend Principle**: When in doubt, ask myself "How would I act toward my closest friend in this situation?"

5. **Client Intimacy**: It all comes down to the depth of the relationship. The closer the relationship, the more likely it is to last and grow, and the less susceptible the client is to competitor's offerings.

6. **Be Bold and Memorable**: The enemy of success is bland and boring.

7. **Meaningful Life Experience or Nothing**: No one gets to waffle. All clients must be full participants.

CHAPTER 3: TRAINING DAY TWO

The next morning Bill walked in around 9am. According to his training itinerary, Bill was supposed to spend the day at one of the incoming call centers. The group he was visiting managed current client accounts. Each current client was assigned to a specific client representative in this call center. Bill walked into the building just as Mr. Free's daily announcements began:

"Good morning everyone. Yesterday was a great day for the outside sales department. I was told that two members of the sales team, Harry Cash and Jon Thrasher, had their best days ever, yesterday. That's fantastic! Despite these records, I am going to have to give the 'hero of the day' award to a member of Mr. Quest's call center team. Richard Levin received a call from Patterson Trucking Company. Chris Patterson stated that he was 'shorted' several parts in his delivery that were crucial to their business. This was a huge problem for Chris because some of his clients were blocked from ordering his products until he received these particular parts. Richard sprang into action to fix the problem. He personally went to distribution to make sure the parts were available. After loading a dolly with the parts that Patterson needed, he went to the delivery department to secure a truck. Unfortunately, the delivery department was not going to have a truck available for a number of hours. Always focused on creating a meaningful life experience for his clients, Richard jumped into his personal car and delivered the part to Patterson Trucking. Anyone who sees Richard today, please take a moment to thank him for his efforts. This is Richard's fourth 'Hero of the Day' award.

In other news, two employees and a client have birthday's today—Susan Peters in sales, Garrett Reagan in deliveries, and our good friend, Page Pace, at Broward Electronic.

That's all I have at this time. As always, let's create a meaningful life experience today.

Bill was blown away by two of the items mentioned in the announcements. First, he could not believe that a person in the call center was allowed to pull items out of inventory and then personally deliver them to a client. It seemed to Bill that this practice would create a logistical nightmare. They would have to reduce the inventory, correct the earlier paperwork, find someone to fill in for the call center employee while he made the run, reimburse gas in an employee's car, etc. He had never worked at a company who gave employees this level of autonomy and authority, nor had he heard of a company who had the infrastructure to allow this kind of client service to occur. While he was intrigued, the whole thing scared Bill a little bit. From his past experience, he could see all kinds of issues emerging as a result of running a business in this way.

Bill was on his way to meet Mr. Quest, the head of the call center. As Bill walked through a bevy of call center employees conversing with clients, one conversation caught his attention. He overheard an employee who seemed to be wasting time, talking on the phone with friends, instead of doing his job.

"You're wrong, man, Kansas City is going to win the division this year; just because they are 1-3 does not mean that they've fallen apart," Bill overheard the employee emphatically proclaiming over the phone.

Clear of the employee's vision, Bill listened to the conversation for about ten minutes. After the conversation ended Bill spoke to the employee. "What's you name?" Bill asked.

"Christian!"

"My name is Bill, and I'm training to become the VP of marketing," Bill stated with authority in his voice, "Are you taking a break or something?" Bill inquired calmly.

"No, why do you ask?" Christian replied

"I overheard you talking about football on the phone for the last ten minutes."

"Actually," Christian responded while glancing down at his watch, "it was more like a half hour."

"Don't you feel like that was a waste of time?" Bill said in a tone that reeked of wrong doing.

"No, not at all. I was talking to Ted Lamb over at Character Counts; he is one of our long time clients." Christian responded calmly.

"So, what does that have to do with your job?" Bill continued.

"Ted calls me every Monday to discuss the previous day's football games; he's been doing so for the past three years. I'm the first call he makes every Monday. Talking football with Ted is part of my pledge to create a meaningful life experience for my clients. As long as Ted calls me every Monday, I am doing my job."

While taking in what Christian had just told him, Bill noticed that the walls of Christian's cubicle were filled with all kinds of certificates and other items. The back wall was filled with lapel pins that seemed to go back years.

"That's the 'hero of the day' lapel pin?" Bill asked while pointing at the back wall.

"Yes, I have won 'hero of the day' 22 times since I started working here, seven years ago," Christian said with pride in his voice, "Additionally, I was employee of the year, three years ago," Christian continued, while pointing at the trophy on the corner of his desk.

"Can you tell me about the rest of these things?" Bill inquired.

"Sure, these 'Thank You' cards are from Mr. Free, Every time you submit an idea for improving the company; you get a note from Mr. Free."

Bill took one of the cards off the wall and looked at it. He was surprised when he started reading the thank you card and realized that is was not a pre-printed card, but a handwritten note from Mr. Free himself.

"So, you submit your ideas for improvements to your manager?" Bill asked.

"Sure, we all do; it is part of our job," Christian replied, "Except we don't give them to our managers; we put them into the 'idea box' you walked past on your way over here and Mr. Free's assistant collects them each day."

"So what is the story with all of the New York Mets stuff?" Bill continued while jotting down a few notes in his notebook.

"I'm a huge Mets fan, and I have been collecting this stuff for most of my life," Christian replied.

"No one complains that your cubicle looks like this? It is pretty unprofessional," Bill remarked.

"Yeah, we don't really care about that so much. All of our cubicles represent our individual personalities. We bring our identities to work with us. This is far more important then sterile professionalism. One of the keys to building quality relationships is letting people know who you are. This is a culture that promotes personal expression. Not only does everyone in the office know I am a Mets fan, but all of my clients know it as well. Also, as part of our effort to increase client intimacy, I am the account rep for most of the clients who are Mets fans."

"So, what's with the baseball lineup on your desk?" Bill continued, writing vigorously while Christian spoke.

"This is my fantasy league line-up. I'm part of a baseball fantasy league with employees throughout the company and a few of my clients. It's a lot of fun. I'm currently in fourth place."

Bill was about to leave when he noticed a miniature red statue not more then four inches high in the top left corner of Christian's desk. The statue had a silly looking guy hitting himself on top of the head.

"What's that thing?" Bill inquired pointing at the statue.

"Oh this," Christian said with a laugh, "This is the 'Mistake of the Year Award' for 2001."

"What?" Bill replied, puzzled.

"You've heard about the 'hero of the day' award, right?" Christian asked.

Bill nodded.

"The 'hero of the day' is recognition for the most successful effort in creating a meaningful life experience for a client or employee. This statue, however, is the 'woody award', named after Mr. Free's dog; it's given to the employee who makes the biggest mistake while attempting to create a meaningful life experience for a client or employee."

"So you were rewarded for making a mistake?" Bill asked.

"Not just a mistake, a mistake while trying to advance the company's mission... a mistake while trying to build a meaningful life experience. I was working with the Johnson Group when I... hang on," Christian reached for the phone. After talking for about a minute he told the person on the other end of the line to hang on and turned to Bill, "Bill, I am going to have to take this call; it was good talking with you. Mr. Quest is down that hall, to the left."

Mr. Quest's office was a small, open space with glass across the entire front wall. On his door was a sign that read:

"Thank you for coming to my office; please look through my window NOW. If I am on the phone or in a meeting please write your name and phone extension on the white board on the door, and I will get with you later. Otherwise, feel free to come

on in. That is unless you are a University of Colorado football fan, in which case you can never step foot in my office :) "

Bill looked into the office and saw Mr. Quest writing a note so he figured it must be alright to walk in.

"Hey, how ya doin!" Mr. Quest exclaimed while jumping to his feet to greet Bill. "I've heard so many good things about you, Bill; it is great to finally meet you."

"Good to meet with you, too, Mr. Quest, I've been here less than an hour and I already have a bunch of questions for you."

"Great Bill, I hope I can give you some helpful answers. I'm a regular part of the three day training process and, as such, I generally just keep working and let the trainee follow me around. I've found that you learn more from watching me work than you would from a long, drawn out lecture. Just take good notes, and I promise I will get to all of your questions before the day is over."

Just as Bill was about to ask his first question, he was interrupted by Mr. Quest shouting toward an employee walking by his office. "Hey, Christina, come in here!" Mr. Quest bellowed.

"I heard a rumor that you had four client 'up sells' yesterday." Mr. Quest stated with a big smile on his face.

"Yes, that's true," Christina passively replied, blushing slightly.

"That's awesome!" Mr. Quest responded, "Keep up the great work."

Christina said thank you and headed on her way.

....

"Bill, I'm supposed to teach you about creating a meaningful life experience for employees. I will be teaching you six keys to cultivating a meaningful experience for employees. You just witnessed the first one. Write down the following: 'all humans crave attention'. Employees will always act in a manner that will get them greater attention in the future; therefore, it is critically important that you give attention to the actions that match the result you are wishing to see repeated. Every single time I see an employee doing something that matches the company mission, I immediately praise the action.

One of the most common mistakes that I see managers in other companies make is failing to give consistent attention to those who are doing their jobs well. So many managers spend more time giving attention to people who are doing their jobs poorly. When you do this, you tell your employees that the way to get attention is to do something wrong. I give attention to those who are consistently exhibiting the behaviors that lead to meaningful life experiences. You can never over-recognize great work. I believe in celebrating excellence, and I do so every chance I get, not just because it is crucial to employee success, but also because it makes my job more fun. As a manager, if you will frequently and consistently celebrate the positives you create a culture that is constantly positive and very productive. Additionally, you should be very specific about the action that you are rewarding. This is crucial to guaranteeing that the behavior will be repeated in the future."

"Anyhow," Mr. Quest continued, "I have an employee coming in to discuss an issue in just a minute, and "Would you please move over to the seat against the wall so that she can sit in front of me?"

Almost like clockwork, a woman in her early twenties named Sarah came in to see Mr. Quest. Sarah was a woman who had a very open, bubbly personality. Before Bill even left his chair, Sarah noticed him in the corner and introduced herself.

Mr. Quest jumped in, "Sarah is one of the stars of the call center: she was the company 'hero of the day' for her second time, three weeks ago. She has been with us for about two years," "Sarah, do you mind if Bill observes our conversation? Mr. Quest asked, "He's in training."

Sarah nodded that she did not mind and took her seat in front of Mr. Quest's desk.

"So, what's going on Sarah?" Mr. Quest asked.

"Well, I want to talk about something that happened last week. I lost an 'exceptional service credit' because the survey team made an error in documenting their call to Nancy Briley. The survey team claimed that Nancy only gave me a 7 out of 10. I spoke to Nancy this morning, and she told me that she gave me a 10 out of 10. I think the survey folks made a mistake."

"Oh, alright," he responded calmly. Mr. Quest went over to his computer and pulled up Nancy Briley's phone number from his client list. He hit the speaker phone button and waited for Nancy's office to answer. After going through the Briley Consulting phone system Nancy answered.

"Hey Nancy, this is Steve Quest over at AceCalc. How're you doing?"

"Great Steve, long time, no talk. How're the kids?"

"Great, thanks for asking, how is your volleyball team doing?"

"We have three wins and three losses right now. We lost to the team with Natalie Marchetti from Palmer Inc; she is really good, you know she played in college."

"Yeah, she's a good all around athlete; she and I are on a co-ed softball team together."

"Steve, I would love to spend more time catching up, but I have an appointment waiting in the lobby. What can I do for you?"

"Sarah, your account rep, told me that you were misquoted when the survey team called you last week."

"Yes Steve: I love Sarah. She is one the best AceCalc reps I've ever had."

"So on a scale of 1-10, what score would you give her on overall client experience?"

"Fifteen!" Nancy replied.

"Thanks, Nancy, I just wanted to straighten things out. Thanks for your help."

"It was good talking with you Steve, I just joined a new committee over at AceCalc, so I will stop by and see you the next time I'm in the building. Gotta run. Bye."

Steve hit the speakerphone button, ending the call and then turned back toward Sarah. "So you want your 'exceptional service credit' back?" Mr. Quest asked with a smirk.

"Yes, I'm really close to a bonus and I can't spare any credits."

With Sarah still sitting in the office, Mr. Quest called the survey department, explained what had happened, and had them make the change on Sarah's report. After the call Mr. Quest asked Sarah, "Have I fully addressed your issue?" Sarah nodded in the affirmative.

Mr. Quest continued, "Is this issue still blocking your ability to provide a meaningful life experience for your clients?" Sarah said "no".

"Does this issue in any way affect your own meaningful life experience with the company?"

Sarah smiled and said, "No. Thanks Mr. Quest"

After a few more minutes of small talk, Sarah headed back to her desk, and Mr. Quest waved for me to move back to the front chair.

"I'm impressed that you took the time to change that for her," Bill remarked.

"That's my job, Most of my time is spent creating a meaningful life experience for the employees in my department," Mr. Quest replied.

"Why did you ask her those questions at the end?" Bill inquired.

"Every employee throughout the company finishes meetings that way. It guarantees that issues that hindering each employee's ability to do their jobs are fully resolved. Miscommunications block employees from their meaningful life experience. We do everything we can to make sure that this does not occur. This brings me to another one of the concepts that I want to teach you."

Bill grabbed his pen and got ready to take some more notes. He was only half way though his second day and he had already taken over ten pages of notes.

"Here at AceCalc we feel that the worst sin of management is making an employee feel powerless. When employees feel that they are powerless, it leads to frustration. One of the top reasons that good employees leave companies is because of frustration. When former employees are asked why they left a company, it almost always has something to do with situations which block their abilities to do quality work."

As Mr. Quest said 'block' he held his hands up and made a quotation sign, giving the impression that this was a commonly used phrase within the culture.

"In our organization, employees are required to address anything that blocks their ability to create a meaningful life experience for our clients. If they do not immediately address anything that is blocking them from doing their duties, they are in breach of their employee contract. As the department manager, it's my responsibility to do whatever's necessary in order to fix the 'blockage' so that the employee can get back to her clients. Employees are always in charge of their client's experience. I'm in charge of giving them the tools to do whatever's necessary to maximize the meaningful life experience for each client."

Mr. Quest continued, *"This brings me to the third key; every employee knows what's expected of them in clear, objective terms. One of the keys to creating a meaningful experience for employees is giving them a path on which to walk. To get the most out of your employees, you must clearly identify their job duties and responsibilities and match their responsibilities, goals, recognition and compensation directly to job objectives. Here at AceCalc, all employees know that they are in charge of their own success. They understand that the harder they work the more rewards they will receive. It's all up to them. This is very empowering to the employees and the entire organization."*

Bill thought about the first company he had worked for in his youth. He recalled that people were promoted and praised more for kissing up to the boss and playing politics than for doing their jobs well. In fact, every company he had ever worked for promoted people more based more on internal politics than job performance.

Due to his past experience, Bill was a little skeptical about what Mr. Quest was saying. He made a note in his notebook, "watch for examples of politics at work in the organization."

Just as Bill finished writing, he saw Mr. Free walking up to the door. Bill was amazed as he watched Mr. Free pick up the white board marker to write his name on Mr. Quest's door, just as other employees are asked to do. Bill assumed that Mr. Free wouldn't bother to obey a note written on a lower level employee's door; after all, Mr. Free was the CEO. Just as Mr. Free was about to walk away, Mr. Quest caught his eye and waved him in.

"I didn't want to interrupt your meeting," Mr. Free remarked with a smile.

"No big deal; we're just chatting. What's up Mr. Free?" Mr. Quest asked.

"Didn't Shawn Retzer have his big bike race this past weekend?" Mr. Free asked Mr. Quest.

"Yes, he came in third; I spoke to him about it this morning."

"Great, I wrote him a note of congratulations, and I'm going to drop it by his desk." Mr. Free stated with a warm smile.

"Go ahead; he'll appreciate that," Mr. Quest said with a nod as Mr. Free burst back through the door to give Shawn his note.

"Mr. Free is involved so closely with every member of the team," Mr. Quest said with a smile.

"Yeah," Bill responded half-heartedly, obviously lost in his thoughts. Bill could not imagine the head of a 200-person company knowing about a single employee from his call center having a bike race. He thought, "Doesn't treating employees in this manner usurp his authority as the boss?"

"I think I walked by Shawn's cubicle earlier, I remember seeing a cubicle with pictures of bike races all over the walls," Bill recollected.

"Yeah, Shawn is a professional cyclist, He is one of the top cyclists in the state," Mr. Quest responded.

"Is he part-time?" Bill asked.

"No, he is a full time employee," Mr. Quest responded, "Why do you ask?"

"I figured he would need time to train," Bill responded.

"Oh, we built his schedule around his training regimen. Part of creating a meaningful life experience for employees is matching their work schedules with their life interests. Shawn trains in the mornings and comes to work around noon. He then works from noon to around 9:00pm. He also gets time off about four times a year to go to major races. All of our employees work a schedule that matches their lifestyle. This brings me to another key concept to creating a meaningful life experience for employees. As you can see from looking at the individual offices throughout the building, we want people to bring their identities to work. As a manager, one of my responsibilities is creating a culture in which people feel comfortable being themselves at work. Each employee's personal life and work life should be seamless. We want to create a feeling of belonging. Do you see the cubicle right outside my window with all of the Harry Potter stuff? That belongs to Stacy Kemper. She's not here today because she's waiting in line to see the sneak preview of the new Harry Potter movie that's coming out this weekend. Most companies would never give someone the time to do something like wait in line for a movie. Not only is she doing it, but people are calling her every few hours to see how she is

doing. It's about being part of people's lives rather than a life interrupting their lives.

After spending a minute or two jotting down notes on identity, Bill asked if it was a good time to go over some of the questions he had from earlier in the day. Mr. Quest glanced at the clock on his desk and told Bill that they only had ten minutes before the weekly department staff meeting. Bill hastily flipped through his notes to find the one or two items he wanted to discuss the most.

"This morning I met a gentleman who had received some recognition for submitting ideas to Mr. Free on how to improve the company. How does that system work?" Bill asked.

"Great question. Did you learn about the client contract during your first day of training?" Mr. Free asked.

Bill nodded in the affirmative.

"All of the employees at AceCalc have also signed a contract; it's called the Team Member Contract. In this contract, each employee makes two promises. The first promise is called 'responsibility for the meaningful life experience'. This is a commitment to do everything possible to contribute to the company mission thus creating a meaningful life experience. The way this promise most often comes into play, is in making sure that nothing blocks any employee from providing a meaningful life experience for those you are responsible for touching. It is every employee's responsibility to address any hindrance at the company. This may include a miscommunication among employees, a computer system issue, or even a survey issue like the one you saw me address earlier. If any employee does not take steps to address a hindrance to performing their job duties they are responsible

for the result it creates. This is what 'responsibility for the meaningful life experience' means. The second promise is called 'one more step'. This promise addresses the question that you asked. Every employee promises to always look for ways to improve the way the company does business, regardless of the department they work in or their time with the company. Along with receiving recognition, each employee has incentives that motivate them to look for ways to improve the company. This employee promise is linked to one of the key concepts that I want to teach you. Here at AceCalc, we believe that 'all brains matter'. Mr. Free fervently believes that one of the keys to staying on top is pulling in as much brainpower as possible.

Mr. Quest looked at his cluttered bulletin board for a few seconds and untacked a little piece of paper that said,

"Here at AceCalc every mind matters. Just remember, Einstein was a patent clerk"

Mr. Quest tacked the quote back up on the bulletin board and looked around for his meeting notes.

"The staff meeting starts in a few minutes, follow me," Mr. Quest remarked as he hastily looked around his office, making sure he did not forget anything.

They walked through the call center department on their way to the meeting room. As Bill walked past each cubicle he paid special attention to the items on each person's walls. In addition to the never ending plagues, thank you cards, and other recognition Bill noticed that people really did bring their identities to work. You could tell a lot about each person just by walking past their cubicles.

About 50-feet from the meeting room Bill started to here a clamor of laughter and loud talking. Mr. Quest smiled and said, "That's the group; they're always very spirited." Mr. Quest stopped in the door and raised his hand. The group instantly stopped talking and looked at Mr. Quest.

"Who are we?" Mr. Quest yelled with exuberance.

"Team Quest!" the team yelled back at the top of their lungs.

"What do we do?" Mr. Quest yelled again.

"We protect the exterior!"

"How do we do it?" Mr. Quest yelled one last time while walking to the front of the room.

"Meaningful Life Experience." The group yelled back as they sat down.

Only a minute into the meeting Bill could tell this was not like any office meeting he had ever seen. He was used to employees slowly walking in to meeting rooms as if the meeting was a burden.

"All right guys, what do you think the team numbers will be this week?" Mr. Quest asked.

Immediately team members started shouting out numbers between 85 and 95. After about 30 seconds of building the suspense, Mr. Quest announced, "We went up two points to 88%." The entire team started cheering as if they were at a sporting event and their favorite team had just scored.

"Don't forget, if we get to 90% by the end of the month we'll go out for pizza and bowling," Mr. Quest added while the team cheered and gave each other "high-five's. "In other good news," Mr. Quest continued, "we had 38 'up sells' this week which brings our total for the month up to 61. This is 14 more then we had last year at this time. Congratulations team! I have quite a bit of individual recognition to hand out today. First, I would like to recognize Richard for being the company 'hero of the day' today." Just as Mr. Quest finished his comment the team went over and playfully patted Richard on the back. While laughing, Richard covered his head while several dozen hands hit him on the back. Mr. Quest continued, "As if this was not enough, Richard also led the team with eight 'up sells' this week. I would also like to recognize Niki for having a personal best of five 'up sells' this week." The team jumped up once again and patted both team members on the back. "Mr. Free received a great letter from The Janis Group praising Shannon. The letter is very long so I will only touch on the key points, but it will be on the board outside my office after this meeting. Additionally, a second copy is on the board outside of Mr. Free's office right now with a comment from Mr. Free written on it."

Mr. Quest sat down for the first time and waited for the group to quiet, "Guys, this has been a great week for our department. Your efforts have made a significant contribution to the company. In gross dollars, the 'up sells' we have sold so far this month will amount to a 3-5% increase in gross company billing for the month. This is an outstanding impact. Even though it has become common place in our department, we should, also, never forget that the best contribution we have made to our bottom line is 'zero lost clients' for the month and only one lost client this year."

Mr. Quest got back up clapped his hands together once, gave the group a big smile and said, "Alright team, let's keep up the great work and have an even better week next week."

Picking up his stuff, from the front desk and walking toward the door he turned and, once again, shouted toward the group:

"Who are we?"

"Team Quest!" "

What do we do?"

"We protect the exterior!"

"How do we do it?"

"Meaningful Life Experience."

Bill followed Mr. Quest back to his office.

....

It was around 5:30pm, and Bill still had a lot of questions to ask. Mr. Quest checked his email and daily calendar and then asked Bill if he wanted to grab a beer at a nearby sports bar. Bill jumped at the chance to spend a little more time learning from Mr. Quest. They jumped into Mr. Quest's car and headed toward the bar.

A few minutes later, they pulled up to a place that Bill had not previously noticed. The bar was called "The Free Zone".

"Is this place named after Mr. Free?" Bill asked."Yes," Mr. Quest replied, "It was started about ten years ago by a retired AceCalc employee. Almost all of the bar customers are employees and clients of AceCalc."

Bill and Mr. Quest entered the bar to a spattering of hellos. After Mr. Quest introduced Bill to a handful of other AceCalc employees they sat down at a two top table in the corner. "So what did you think of the meeting?" Mr. Quest asked.

"It was the most positive office meeting I have ever attended: Your team is really fired up," Bill responded, "It was also one of the shortest meetings I have ever witnessed. You got through everything in about twenty five minutes."

"Yeah, that was a typical meeting for my department. Sometimes we have more discussion on the methods that team members are using to create meaningful life experiences for clients. Typically, when all of our numbers are positive, such as today, I focus all my efforts on recognition, job value, and reiterating the mission. These are the quickest meetings. When numbers are down, I concentrate more on training and focus."

"What do you mean by 'job value'?" Bill asked.

"This is another one of the keys to a meaningful employee experience that I want to teach you. It is very important that every employee understands how their daily efforts impact the company's overall success. Every chance I get, both with the group and with individual employees, I discuss how each employees efforts effect the overall company. In order to get the most out of employees they must feel like they are valuable contributors to the organization. First, if they see themselves as inconsequential to the organization they will not put as much care into their jobs on a daily basis. Second, understanding their importance to the organization has a positive effect on their self-worth.

Bill jotted down some notes and then followed up immediately, "You also mentioned 'reiterating the mission'; I noticed that you did that at the beginning and at the end of the meeting. Why did you do this?"

"We feel that it is very important to constantly reiterate the company mission. You probably noticed Mr. Free does this at the end of the morning announcements every day. Additionally, every category of recognition one can receive within the company, including compensation and promotions, is directly linked to how well they implement the company mission. In a lot of companies the mission is a dusty plaque on the wall that no one ever reads. They take it for granted that employees understand and are committed to the company mission.

"I have a story about this issue. Last year, I went to visit my brother in Los Angeles. He is a partner in an accounting firm. While I was there, I spent some time with eight of his employees. During my discussion with the employees, I asked them to each answer the following question: *'What is your company ultimately trying to accomplish?'* I received five different answers from eight people.

"It is critically important to an organization's success that every employee have the same perception of the company's mission and goals. Mr. Free feels that out-of-site is out-of-mind. Each employee hears the mission, in one way or another, several times a day. They understand that the 'meaningful life experience' is what we are all about. This cannot be taken for granted. By the way, I call this concept 'mission ad nausea'."

As Mr. Quest finished his thought, a man, who appeared to be in his 70's, walked up to say hello.

"What's up Quest, you breaking in a new trainee?" the man said patting Mr. Quest on the back.

"Hey Lou, This is Bill; he's in his second day of training. Bill, this is Lou; he washes the delivery trucks," Mr. Quest responded.

After shaking Bill's hand, Lou spent a few minutes talking about some of his experiences with the company. Lou was a retired police officer looking for something to do when he joined the company three years ago. Although he was only part time, it was obvious that he was very involved in the company culture. In addition to his job, he umpired for the company softball league and mentored some of the company's younger employees. The three of them spoke for about ten minutes before Lou saw some guys that he wanted to talk with come in the front door. He shook both their hands and headed on his way.

"How do you know Lou so well?" Bill asked.

"Lou is a great guy. We met while helping at a charity event last year."

Bill looked down for a second, wondering how to phrase his next question without being offensive.

"I have noticed that a lot of employees at different levels of the company are friends."

"Well… this is the last of the key concepts I wanted to teach you. This one will be hard for you to understand after working with a lot of more traditional companies. We don't have hierarchy at AceCalc. We're all at the same level. No one really works for anyone else. We all work to achieve the same purpose."

"But you have employees; you're the head of a department," Bill responded, confused.

"Well sure, my task is to manage a call center, but that's not my job, my job is creating a meaningful life experience for employees and clients. I know this is hard for people with experience in more traditional companies to grasp, but we feel the negatives associated with a rigid hierarchy far outweigh the positives. Additionally, we just don't understand how a company class system in any way matches our company's purpose. Our company is completely flat. Everyone does their part to help create a meaningful life experience.

Bill couldn't believe what he was hearing; he couldn't fathom a company with no hierarchy. This went against all of his past experiences. Just before Bill was about to follow up with more questions Mr. Quest interrupted, "I have found that the best way to learn this concept is to simply watch the company function. I used to try and explain it to every new employee and found that they just can't picture it until they see it in action. Anyhow, I really have to get home now. I hope I was helpful.

"Yes, I am overwhelmed by what I have seen and heard," Bill replied with a hint of enthusiasm.

"Great, I think you will really learn a lot tomorrow, too. The lessons on the management side really put the puzzle together. "Mr. Quest looked down at his watch, tossed some money onto the table, and hastily walked to the door with Bill following. Mr. Quest dropped Bill off at his car, shook his hand, and headed on his way.

Bill tossed his notes in the passengers' seat and headed home. This time he did not even stop to eat. As soon as he got home he sat down and went through all of the notes he had taken that day. Just like the night before, he went through all of his notes and summarized them into one page.

Keys to Creating Meaningful Life Experience for Employees

1. **All Humans Crave Attention:**Constantly celebrate positive behavior.

2. **Identity at work:** Create a culture in which people feel comfortable being themselves. Home lives and work lives should be seamless.

3. **All Brains Matter:** Every employee must contribute ideas in order for the company to grow.

4. **No Powerlessness:** Never let an employee feel powerless.

   - Employees should always feel like they have full ability to perform their job duties.

   - Employees should always feel that they are in complete control of their future.

   - Employees should always feel that they are being treated fairly.

   - All employee recognition and compensation should be clear, consistent, and as objective as possible.

   - Everyone must understand where they stand and what they must do to move ahead.

5. **Reiterate mission ad nausium**: You can never overstate the mission.

6. **Job Value**: All employees must understand how their job impacts the company's overall success. The more important they feel the more care they will put into their daily efforts.

CHAPTER 4: TRAINING DAY THREE

Bill went into his third day of training a little skeptical. Although he was excited and intrigued by what he had seen so far, he still believed that there had to be a trick. After all, Bill had been in the business world for over 25 years and he had never seen a company doing business remotely like AceCalc. Fraught with cynicism from years of indoctrination in traditionally run organizations, Bill went into the third day of training searching for rotten wood. Even though all of the lower employees he had met thus far had bought into the company's mission and the concepts he learned in his first two days of training, he expected to find that upper management operated far more like the companies he had worked for in the past.

Bill arrived at work around 8:45am. After spending a few minutes chatting with a few employees as he walked through the building, Bill entered a small boardroom just a few feet down the hall from Mr. Free's office. Bill was to start the day observing the executive team's weekly board meeting.

As he walked into the boardroom he was greeted by the gentleman that he was replacing as Vice President of Marketing. Tom Promise was a tall man in his late 50's with salt and pepper hair. Tom had a very calm and unassuming demeanor.

"Bet you are glad to be retiring", Bill said, attempting to make small talk and break the silence in the room.

"No big deal," Tom replied, "I've been here for a long time. I was Mr. Free's seventh employee. I'm leaving my position, but I will still be around. I am just changing to part time status. Also, if you like volleyball you will probably see me around the courts."

Tom's attitude toward retirement was quite different then Bill has seen from people in previous companies for which he had worked. Most people Bill had seen retire counted the days, and often even the seconds, before their last day. Now that Bill had met about half a dozen AceCalc employees, he was really starting to notice how closely each one was tied to the company.

Gradually, the other five vice presidents and Mr. Free made their way into the meeting room.

"Before we get started I want to introduce everyone to Bill Nettles. Bill will be taking Tom's place as Vice President of Marketing. Bill is in his third day of training today. Please make him feel at home as we do with all new employees," Mr. Free remarked.

The group went around the table and introduced themselves to Bill. After telling a joke to start the meeting, Mr. Free pulled six copies of the agenda out of a folder and passed them around the table.

"Are any employees feeling under challenged right now?" Mr. Free asked the group.

"One of my guys is looking for added responsibilities. He has been doing his current job for about three years and he is ready for a new challenge," Tom stated.

"Where does he want to go?" Mr. Free asked.

Tom turned to Tia Blackley, vice president over logistics and the call center, "Tia, do you have an opening for an assistant director level employee, I think my guy would be great for in a position like that?" Tom asked.

"Tom, let me talk to a few of my managers and see what I can do for you. I was thinking about creating a new position in processing that might be ideal. I will come by and see you this afternoon."

"Any other employees currently under challenged?" Mr. Free asked the group.

Mr. Free waited for a moment and then went on to the next item on his agenda.

"Are there any blocks to front end employees creating meaningful life experiences for clients?" Mr. Free continued.

"I was speaking to Ms. Happy yesterday and she told me that we have a request from Calvin Air Supply to deliver before 9:00am starting on the first of the month. They have changed some of their internal processes and they need to start doing inventory in the mornings instead of the afternoon," Tia stated to the group.

"Is something blocking us from filling this request?" Mr. Free asked.

"Yes, we have so many morning deliveries that I would have to add a truck or a part time driver in order to get their products delivered by 9:00am. We don't have any open slots before 11:00am right now."

"Does anyone have any ideas on this one?" Mr. Free asked the group.

After some small talk Vice President of Operations Robert Champion spoke up. "Does Jimmy Norton's company still get morning deliveries?" Robert asked Tia.

"I think so, let me call Ms. Happy and make sure," Tia responded.

Tia picked up the speaker phone in the middle of the table and called Ms. Happy. After confirming that Jimmy Norton's company still received morning deliveries, Robert continued.

"Jimmy, Brenda Calvin, and I are on a softball team together. If I'm not mistaken, I do not believe that Jimmy still needs to get deliveries that early in the morning. I think if we asked him he would let us move his deliveries back to noon. Delivery time is no longer as important to his business as it was a few years back. Let's get him on the phone, he will not mind."

To Bill's amazement, Robert called Jimmy Norton and asked him if he would be willing to move his delivery time back three hours.

"Hey Jimmy," Robert began, "I need a favor from you."

"What's up Robert," Jimmy responded. "Brenda, on our softball team, needs to move her delivery time up a few hours, and we don't have the trucks to do it. Didn't you tell me that you no longer need to get deliveries before 9:00am?"

"Yea, as long as I can stay before noon I'll be fine. I used to run tight on some inventory, but we haven't had that issue in over a year. Go ahead and swap her time with mine. Tell her if I run out of something I will come knocking on her door." Jimmy said jokingly.

"Thanks Jimmy, I will see you on Friday night for our game." Robert replied. They chatted for a few seconds longer and said goodbye.

"Great," Mr. Free said calmly, "we were able to fix a problem without increasing our expenses purely based purely on the quality of the relationship that we have developed with two of our clients. Great job Robert!"

As Mr. Free went from issue to issue Bill had to admit that he was completely wrong about what he would see in the senior staff meeting. Bill expected the senior staff meeting to be similar to the meetings he had seen at previous employers. After observing the senior group he realized that this part of the way AceCalc did business was as unique as every other part of the business. As Bill sat and listened he observed the senior staff consistently applying the company's mission as they discussed each issue with openness, efficiency, and cunning effectiveness.

Bill sat in the corner taking pages of notes while the group discussed dozens of issues. A little while later the meeting concluded. After shaking everyone hand and leaving the meeting room Bill sat down on a bench in the hallway to collect his thoughts.

He decided to review his notes for a few minutes before going to his next meeting. As he went through his notes he could see where Mr. Free applied many of the same principles that Bill has seen other managers extol. Mr. Free showered the group with recognition. Everyone in the room was praised for something. This was by far the most human and personal executive business meeting Bill has ever witnessed. Mr. Free frequently went off point to discuss issues outside of work with each of the team members. However, the entire hour-long meeting was centered on four simple concepts, three of which went directly to the company mission:

1. **How can we help front end employees improve the meaningful life experience for clients?**

2. How can we improve the meaningful life
   experience for employees?

3. How can I (Mr. Free) improve your (the vice
   presidents) meaningful life experience?

The only concept Mr. Free discussed that Bill had not previously been taught was "under challenged employees". Bill made a note to ask about this concept when he met with Tom later in the day.

After reviewing the notes Bill took a moment to sit back and relax. For the first time he was starting to feel more excited then anxious about his new job. Many of the stresses he had endured for decades did not exist at AceCalc. Although the meeting was not at the same heightened pitch as the meeting he had observed the previous day in the call center, Bill was struck by the positive and calm demeanor of the executive staff. Bill was accustomed to high stress board meetings full of politicking. Bill had spent hours of his professional life sitting in these types of meetings trying to spin the reality of the day to make himself look as good as possible to his superiors. Here, there was no pressure or political games. The discussion was very open and productive. The tone of the meeting was calm and purposeful. The meeting was definitely an example of the 'no hierarchy' concept he had been taught by Mr. Quest the day before. Although he was only in his third day of training, for the first time he started to really believe that this was a company with a truly different way of doing business at every level. Sitting back in a big leather chair, Bill felt a relaxed calm come over his body.

....

"Bill"

"Bill"

"Hey Bill," Tom Promise repeated with a chuckle. Bill was so deep in thought that he didn't notice Tom walk up.

"Sorry Tom, I was thinking about the executive meeting this morning," Bill explained.

"So what did you think, Bill, was it what you expected?" Tom asked.

"It was unlike any meeting I have ever witnessed. Do you have some time to go over some stuff that was discussed in the meeting?" Bill asked.

"Sure Bill, I planned on spending some time with you this morning. Let's walk over to my office."

The two of them walked through a large open office area where approximately fifteen employees were working together on promotional concepts. Tom stopped toward the back of the office and announced, "Everyone, This is Mr. Nettles, He is going to be the new me." Bill waved to the group and told them that he was looking forward to getting to know each one of them.

"You guys will all get a chance to spend time with Mr. Nettles next week. I know you guys are on a deadline at the moment and I don't want to hold you up. Before I go, who created the last newsletter we sent out to current clients?"

"That was Stephanie," one of the team members said while pointing at a heavy set woman at the back of the room.

"I thought that was one of the best newsletters ever. The presentation was excellent," Tom exclaimed with a smile.

Tom began to clap his hands and the rest of the team followed suit. Stephanie blushed and covered her face.

After grabbing a couple bottles of waters, Bill and Tom made their way to Tom's office. The two sat for over an hour getting to know each other without discussing any business topics. They swapped stories on a broad variety of subjects from history to sports to current events. Finally, after telling stories about AceCalc over the years, Tom preceded to discuss the concepts that drive his management practices.

"Bill, I think by this point you understand that we all work to create a meaningful life experience for our clients, employees, and co-workers. I do not deal with very many "blocking" issues as a part of my job. These issues are usually handled by my directors. I get to spend most of my time working to fulfill people's human needs. I spend a lot of time trying to get people involved in the company's culture. I spend a lot of one on one time getting to know employees. I am always trying to find new ways to tie people's identities into the company. Often this is an effort to match employees with other employees as well as clients who have similar interests. The more I get to know about people the more opportunities I will have to bring people together within the organization. This is one of the most exciting things about my job.

Over the years I have helped start sports leagues, video game clubs, peer counseling groups, and many other types of niches. The more I connect people within the organization the more I contribute to their meaningful life experiences. It's all about fulfilling human needs.

"What do you mean by human needs?" Bill asked.

Tom pulled open his desk drawer and pulled out a laminated business card. As he handed the card to Bill he said, "I think these five human understandings are the key to my role in creating a meaningful life experience for employees and coworkers.

Every human craves:

1. **Social Intimacy**

2. **Identity Acceptance**

3. **A Feeling of Accomplishment**

4. **A Feeling of Appreciation**

5. **A Sense of Belonging**

While looking through the items on the card Bill remembered Mr. Free's question about unchallenged employees from the meeting. "The feeling of accomplishment is what Mr. Free was referring to when he asked if all of the employees felt challenged in their jobs," Bill commented.

"This is a very big issue to Mr. Free," Tom replied, "You may have noticed that challenging employees was the only specific issue Mr. Free brought up outside of the general mission based issues.

Bill nodded in the affirmative.

"Mr. Free believes that one of management's foremost responsibilities is making sure each employee is challenged. He believes that failing in this responsibility is a fatal company mistake. Our employees are our most important asset. Leaving employees unchallenged is a waste of valuable resources. It is simply not tolerated at AceCalc," Tom stated with passion and fire in his eyes.

Just as Bill was about to respond, Tom continued on the challenge issue.

"So many companies have immeasurable talent inside their walls going to waste. One time during morning announcements, Mr. Free said something I will never forget. 'Every employee has more to offer then you think; just remember, Einstein was working as a patent clerk'. Not only does the company suffer when employees are unchallenged, but it is also a direct violation of the company mission. An unchallenged employee is not having a meaningful life experience."

Tom's calm demeanor turned almost to anger during this commentary. It was obvious that this issue fell close to his heart. When talking about companies wasting talented employees, he almost seemed disgusted. Bill looked through his notes for a few minutes while Tom regained his general calm demeanor.

"So you get to know all of your employees very closely?" Bill asked.

"As close as any of my non-AceCalc friends," Tom replied.

After hesitating for a moment Bill asked, "I know that AceCalc is a company with no hierarchy, but do you ever find your close relationship with employees to be a hindrance when you need to address, um, you know, disciplinary issues?"

"Not at all... that is a common misconception that comes out of companies with a lot of politics within their cultures. In a truly mission based company you can never over- humanize the culture. If anything, in the rare occasions that I have to address employee behavior issues, I find the quality of the personal relationships that I have developed to be hugely beneficial to achieving solutions that benefit everyone involved. It's just a different way of doing things."

Once again, before Bill could get a word out Tom had moved on to another concept.

"You are probably used to operating in companies where all of the upper management was "still faced" and unemotional. I call this "sterile management", and I think it is silly and misguided. You can't create a culture in which people feel comfortable to bring their identities to work if you don't let people into your life. As I stated earlier, you can't over humanize a culture, however, you can under-humanize a culture... and most companies do."

Just as Tom finished his thought a sales team member came in to remind him that he had a meeting in five minutes. Tom grabbed some notes that were sitting next to a fish tank on the corner of his desk and headed toward the door. While they walked through the building, Tom made sure that Bill had all of his contact information, shook Bill's hand, and headed into the meeting.

Bill hoped to grab a bite to eat before his next meeting; however, after looking at his wristwatch he realized that he did not have enough time to stop. According to Bill's training itinerary, he was scheduled to attend "A Discussion of Patronage" put on by Mr. Free. Bill headed straight for Mr. Free's office, grabbing an apple and another bottled water on the way.

As he was when Bill came in for his first day of training, Mr. Free was at the front of his office chatting with his receptionist. When Bill walked in, Mr. Free spotted him and greeted him with a warm smile. "I am guessing you have been through a lot over the last day and a half?" Mr. Free asked while shaking Bill's hand.

"Yeah, if I knew a few years ago what I know now, I would have come to AceCalc a long time ago," Bill replied, "I really like the way you guys do things. I still have a lot to learn, but I am intrigued."

"Come on into my office Bill, I just ordered a pizza," Mr. Free stated as he turned and started working toward his office.

Bill walked into Mr. Free's office and was immediately consumed by all of the items on the walls. The office looked like the cubicles Bill has seen in the call center on the first day of training. Everywhere he looked he saw awards, framed thank you letters, pictures, and a million other mementos. Bill felt like he was walking through a company time capsule. One wall was filled with pictures from the previous 25 years. Behind Mr. Free's desk, Bill notices a number of posed group pictures. At first Bill thought that he was looking at each year's staff picture. He focused on the previous year's picture. After noticing that there was at least four hundred people in the picture Bill decided to ask Mr. Free who the people were in the pictures.

"Is this the company picture Mr. Free?" Bill asked.

"Yes, I have them for every year since we started," Mr. Free responded.

"But, I thought we only have about two hundred employees?"

"We do, half of the people in the picture are employees and the other half are clients."

"Clients took the time to be part of the company picture?"

"Of course, why wouldn't they? They are part of the organization."

Bill looked at the pictures for about a minute, grabbed a piece of pizza, and then sat down in one of three chairs in front of Mr. Free's desk.

"Bill, I spend about half an hour with every employee on the last day of their three day training. Instead of filling the trainee with more concepts, policies, and procedures, I try to give them an understanding of how this company came to exist. In your case, Bill, I know you have heard other family members talk about the company over the years, but I still think it is just as important for you to hear the full story, as it would be for any other new hire."

Bill grabbed his notebook, took a swallow of water from his bottle and sat back to listen.

"Before I started AceCalc 25 years ago my professional life was in turmoil. The last two companies I had worked for had both been horribly run.

The first of these companies was a nationally known movie theatre chain. I was the manager of the concessions department. I really enjoyed my job except for one big problem. The general manager was absolutely terrible. He was one of those managers who ran things like a dictator and thought he was completely untouchable. I will never forget him, His name was Jeff Myers. He treated all of his employees like slaves. At one point things got so bad that a number of employees complained to our corporate office. They presented a laundry list of problems to the corporate office including blatant favoritism, sexual harassment, theft, and a number of situations in which the GM had created a hostile work environment.

Two weeks later, he pulled me aside and threatened me by saying that he knew I was the one who had complained and that he was going to make my life miserable. For some reason, I have never been able to piece together, the corporate office didn't fire the GM. As days and months went by he put ever increasing pressure on me. Finally after six months of harassment, he fired me without cause and told me that if I dare challenged the firing he would come after me personally.

On the way out of the building, he followed me, yelling disparaging remarks until I got into my car. It was a horrible experience. The irony was that I had nothing to do with the complaint that was sent to the corporate office. To this day I don't know who it was.

The last company I worked for, before starting AceCalc, was a regional business to business printing company. I was a territory sales person with this company for a little over a year. Up until my last day I was much happier with this company's management then I was with the movie chain. I spent most of my time on the road calling on accounts, so I was able to avoid most of the heavy office politics that were prevalent throughout the culture. Everything seemed to be going fine until around 9:30am on my last day with the company.

I had called into the office from a pay phone to see if I had any messages when my boss got on the line and started asking me about a contract that had been signed the previous week. Through his yelling I was able to deduce that the contract had been written improperly in a way that would cost the company a lot of money. The irony was that I hadn't written the contract in question. I was on the road seeing a client, and my boss had written the contract so that we could get it in before the end of the month. Anyhow, he was worried that he might get fired if he took the blame for the incident, so he lied to his boss and blamed the entire thing on me. I was fired for the incident two hours later by phone. I never even got the opportunity to defend myself.

After I went by the office to get my stuff, I stopped by a café to think. I didn't know what I was going to do next, but I knew that I was tired of working for companies who had no concern for their employees. After about an hour of sitting in a booth staring into space while the world went through my mind, I decided to grab a few napkins and jot down some qualities I would be looking for from my next employer. After about twenty minutes I had jotted notes on about eight napkins without coming to any resolute conclusions.

That day while sitting in the café, I decided that I would start a company that is run the way I think a company should be run. I wanted to do it, not just for myself, but for everyone I knew who was unhappy with their jobs. After going through all of my notes I pulled one more napkin out of the holder and jotted down three concepts that were going to be the cornerstones of the company I would create. To this day, these three concepts are in the forefront of my mind. The first concept is as follows: If you want happy clients you must first have happy employees. In a nutshell, I believe that an unsatisfied employee cannot create a satisfied client. At AceCalc, our goal is client intimacy. I firmly believe that an employee can only create a level of client intimacy equal to their own level of intimacy with the company. If employees are not passionate about the company they will not produce clients who are passionate about the company. It's that simple. Based on this understanding, you can see how true, meaningful client success starts with employee success.

The second concept I jotted down that day was a perception of what I wanted my company to really be about. I wrote the following: **I want my company to be a place where everyone can achieve their individual dreams.** I believe that you are only successful in leading an organization when everyone involved is achieving their dreams together. If any member of our team is not on the path to their personal dreams I am responsible for removing the road blocks.

Over the past 25 years many positive things have happened in this organization. Although we have had many successes that seem grand to someone looking in from the outside, I, personally, never feel more successful than when an employee tells me about things that they are able to achieve in their own lives with the help of the organization.

The last concept I wrote on the napkin that day became the company mission that you have been learning about over the past three days. So Bill, at this point what does creating a meaningful life experience mean to you?

Bill thought for a second and then started, "I think it's about making a positive impact in people's lives every day. It's about the company succeeding through the success of individuals".

"Very good Bill, you have gained a good, basic understanding of the company mission," Mr. Free replied with a smile.

Mr. Free pulled out the center drawer of his desk, grabbed a stack of business card sized pieced of paper and pulled one from under the rubber band holding the stack together. He reached over the desk and handed the card to Bill and told him to put it in his wallet. Bill looked down at the card, which read as follows:

AceCalc Company Mission:
**To achieve long term business success,
you must create a meaningful life experience
for employees, clients, and managers.**

Just a few seconds after handing Bill the mission card, Mr. Free abruptly got up from his desk and told Bill to follow him. Bill shoved the company mission card into his pocket, grabbed all of his stuff, and followed Mr. Free out of the office. After spending a few minutes slowly walking down the hall and sharing family stories, Mr. Free stopped and opened the door to what would be Bill's new office. Bill looked into his new office and then turned back around, to make a comment to Mr. Free. As he turned around he realized that Mr. Free had already walked away.

Bill yelled down the hall, "What do I do now?"

"Well Bill, Tom will come by in about half an hour to introduce you to some of your teammates. In the mean time, why don't you try creating a meaningful life experience for someone," Mr. Free replied with a smile and a wink.

Bill spent the rest of the day walking around his departments and talking to team members. He loved the open, give-and-take culture that AceCalc promoted. In just a few hours he knew many of his team members more personally then he had known co-workers he had worked with for years, at previous companies. After having a conversation with one of the newest sales reps, Bill decided to head home for the day.

At home, Bill grabbed some chicken from the refrigerator and headed to his desk to review his notes from his third day of training. As he had done the previous two days, he summarized his notes into one page of key concepts.

Managing the Mission

1. Do everything you can to match activities within the company to people's individual interests.

2. Every employee must feel challenged in his or her duties and responsibilities at work.

3. Fulfill people's human needs:
   - Social Intimacy
   - Identity Acceptance
   - A Feeling of Accomplishment
   - A Feeling of Appreciation
   - A Sense of Belonging

4. You cannot over humanize an organization.

5. AceCalc is a place where everyone can achieve their dreams. As managers we are successful when those in our organization are successful.

6. An unhappy employee cannot create a happy client. Period.

Company Mission

The Key to AceCalc's success is creating a meaningful life experience for clients, employees, and managers.

BOOK II

LEARNING TO BREATHE

CHAPTER 5

After spending several hours looking through his AceCalc training notes from three and a half years ago, Bill was still baffled. After tediously examining each concept from his training notes, he was unable to find any place where he had changed Mr. Free's policies. With a growing feeling of helplessness consuming his mind, Bill decided to discuss the issue with his team of vice presidents. The next morning at 9:00am, he called all of the vice presidents over to his office for an emergency meeting.

The hand-full of faces that Bill looked upon in the boardroom were far different than the group he met in training three and a half years earlier. Tracy Baldwin, the previous CFO, had been fired for challenging Bill's opinion on a financial issue approximately six months ago. Robert Champion was on his way out. He had already accepted a position with another company after having spent his entire career working for AceCalc. The remaining two vice presidents from Mr. Free's days had become passive and disattached.

"In an attempt to figure out where the company has gone wrong I spent several hours last night going through the policies and procedures that Mr. Free put in place when he ran AceCalc. After reviewing all of our manuals, I have concluded that I have not changed any of the company policies and procedures, over the past two years so the problems in our company must be coming from somewhere else." Bill proclaimed with an air of arrogance.

After giving the speech, Bill leaned forward in his chair and with a challenging tone asks the group, "Do you guys all agree with my conclusions on this issue?"

The group nodded in the affirmative while glancing at each other, wondering if anyone was going to speak up. Speaking up in a board meeting, or any other time, has become quite rare at AceCalc over the past two years.

Bill's aggressive and intimidating nature had sapped all of the legitimate dialogue out of the boardroom. Due to his actions in the past, everyone on the board was afraid to utter any opinion that differed from Bill's. Bill had developed a reputation for responding badly toward anyone who challenged his authority as CEO. Both of the vice presidents who left did so for this reason. The true company culture had gone from creating a meaningful life experience to appeasing Bill's sporadic and hot headed personality.

After half an hour of Bill ranting about all of the ways that employees are not doing their jobs, which he seemed to do every day, Bill adjourned the meeting and headed back to his office. As he walked in the front door, Bill's receptionist flagged him down to tell him about a phone call that had come in a few minutes ago. "Stacy Konley at The Bishop Group called to complain about an issue with deliveries," the assistant told Bill flaccidly.

Bill snatched the note out of her hand and stormed into his office to get the vice president over this department, Tia Blackley, on the phone.

"Why is everyone in the delivery department incompetent?" Bill asked sarcastically.

Rolling her eyes, Tia sat back in her chair and said, "What's the problem Bill?"

"Apparently The Bishop Group is not happy with their driver, and we are doing nothing to help them. Find out what the deal is with this and get back to me today!" Before Tia could say a word Bill had already hung up the phone.

Tia went down to the delivery department to see her new director. Bob is the third director that the delivery department has had in the past two years. Ms. Happy left about a year ago and her replacement left just a few months after being hired. Bob had been promoted to this position about two months ago.

"What's the deal with The Bishop Group?" Tia asked Bob.

"Oh, they're unhappy for two reasons. First of all, they have some billing questions. Secondly, a few items crucial to their business were missing from their order last week."

"What're we doing to fix the problem?" Tia continued.

"We sent two requests to accounting about the billing issues and have yet to hear anything back from them. As far as the missing products, my driver told the call center about it."

"Why didn't the driver see about the products himself?"

"Last time we tried to do that we got the run around in the logistics department. They won't process any packages without a billing copy because all of the guys over there are afraid of disciplinary action."

After a few more minutes of discussion about The Bishop Group issue, Tia decided to go see George Shultz, the manager of logistics and inventory control, as well as Tia's friend over the past few years.

"Hi George, I am trying to resolve an issue with the Bishop Group. I need three boxes of CS943-R replacement tape."

"I would love to give you those items Tia, but Mr. Nettles, our vice president, has written up three people in the department on shrinkage issues, and I was told that I would be in danger of demotion if I gave anyone inventory without a billing slip. I'm really sorry; I'd love to help you, but I just can't. It's gotten to the point that I just don't take any chances anymore. Anytime I go out of my way to help someone it blows up in my face. I don't want to get in trouble," George replied, visually frustrated.

"I completely understand; with all of the restrictions that we deal with these days it's really hard to get anything done between departments anymore. Everyone is afraid of getting in trouble. It's like walking through a minefield; you never know when you're going to step in the wrong place," Tia replied.

After returning to her office. Tia sat at her desk for a few minutes, trying to figure out what to say to Bill. She jotted down few notes and then dialed the number to Bill's office. "Bill, I spoke to the folks in deliveries, and I understand the issue. I will have the missing items on Bishop's next regular delivery, but I'm still working on the accounting issue."

After Tia got finished talking, Bill went into an aggressive rant.

"Why can't we just throw some product on to a delivery truck and get it to the client like we use to do. Doesn't anyone have any initiative around here anymore! You think you can get that done?" Bill asked condescendingly. Bill threw the phone down and muttered to himself, "Idiots, what's wrong with these people? I think I need to replace everyone with people who want to work.

Later in the day, Bill was standing at the back of an elevator when he thought he overheard an employee saying something negative about him to a coworker.

"I don't know; it just seems like it's another bad ownership decision," the employee stated.

As they walked out of the elevator, Bill pulled the employee aside and sternly asked him for his name.

"Brian Lawrence," the employee responded with a confused look on his face.

"What department do you work in?" Bill continued.

"Call Center, Sir."

"Let's go see your director, Brian."

Bill and Brian walked toward the call center. The call center had recently seen some of the highest employee turnover in the entire organization. Mr. Quest left a year ago and most of the employees followed him out the door. The new director's name is Victoria Bolden. She has had the job since Mr. Quest left. Victoria was on the phone with a client when Bill barged in and impatiently tapped his fingers on her desk, waiting for the phone call to end. As soon as Victoria's phone hit the receiver Bill starts to talk. "It seems that this employee has some opinions about the way I run this company."

"What do you mean, Bill?" Victoria asked, attempting to stay calm.

Just as Victoria finished her question Brian's facial expression changed. It's obvious that he doesn't know that the person confronting him is the CEO. Bill never meets with front-end employees like Mr. Free did and many of the newer employees have no idea what he looks like.

"I was in the elevator, and I overheard this person telling a coworker about some bad decision that the owner of the company must have made," Bill continued.

With all of the problems in the company it had become common to hear people complaining about the upper management. Complaining about management had become ingrained in the company culture. It had almost become an icebreaker within the company. If you wanted to build a bond with another employee you would usually go to "The Free Zone" bar after work and complain about management over a few beers.

"So what's your side of the story, Brian?" Victoria asked.

"What side?" Bill interrupted, "Look, I don't have time for a bunch of hand holding; if this employee does not feel like he wants to be here then I am sure we can replace him with someone else!"

Bill left the room and stormed toward his office. After taking a deep breath, Victoria continued her conversation with Brian. "Brian, I know people are going to talk about company issues with coworkers, but you have to pay attention to who is around you."

"Um, I have no idea what he's talking about Ms. Bolden," Brian stated, still confused, "I didn't say anything about the company at all. I was talking to Kaleb about the Washington Redskins football team. I was telling him that the problems with the Redskins were mostly because of bad decisions by their owners."

After taking a moment to process what she'd just heard, Victoria told Brian not to worry about it and sent him back to his desk. After regaining her composure Victoria decided to do some complaining of her own. She called Laura Gaither in the delivery department to discuss what had just taken place. She called the delivery department to talk with Laura Gaither, a long-time friend from high school, about what had just taken place.

"Hello."

"What's up girl?" Victoria replied.

"Just doing deliveries; what's up over in the main building?"

"You'll never believe what just happened to me. I just saw a great example of what we've been saying about Bill Nettles."

"Oh boy, what happened this time, Vic?"

"Bill overheard one of my employees talking about problems with some professional sports team ownership, and he thought that employee was talking about him. Is that not the worst paranoia you have ever heard of?"

"You've got to be kidding; that's hilarious. So then what happened?" Laura continued.

"Well, you know how Bill will freak out if he feels that anyone is challenging his authority."

"Yeah," Laura responded with anticipation.

"This time, he dragged my employee into my office and made an entire scene. It was ridiculous. Bill has some major emotional issues."

"Yeah, Vic, I want to hear the details, but I am getting a call on the other line, I'll talk to you after work."

"See ya girl."

....

So the day goes on at the sinking ship that is AceCalc. It's a typical day; at least what has become a typical day. Bill will receive three more calls from unhappy clients. A frustrated employee or two will head for the door. The battle that is the ever developing political game goes on between employees and departments. Nothing significant really gets done. Everyone simply drones through their days, focused mostly on making themselves look as good as possible to their superiors. The once positive energetic buzz that permeated throughout the organization has given way to whispered conversations and uncalm silence. As the sun moves to the west, Bill sits despondently, looking out the windows of his office.

CHAPTER 6

After another restless night, Bill slowly headed to work. In the past he had been one of the first people in the office, but recently he had started coming in later and later.

Bill took slow, powerless steps down the hall to his office. After getting the day's mail from his office assistant, he grabbed a cup of coffee and unlocked the door to his internal office. After turning on the light, he looked up and notices a man sitting at his desk reading a newspaper.

"How did you get in here?" Bill exclaimed with alarm.

Calmly laying the paper down, the man responded, "I just let myself in."

At a distance the man looked familiar, but Bill couldn't quite make out the face. He cautiously walked closer.

"Can I get some coffee," the man asked Bill.

Just then Bill recognized the intruder; he dropped his briefcase and stared in disbelief. The man sitting at his desk appeared to be company founder, Jack Free.

"What's the problem Bill; not expecting me to visit today?" the man asked jokingly.

"Who are you?" Bill replied.

"It's me, your Uncle, Jack Free." Speechless, Bill started to slowly back peddle toward the door.

"Relax Bill. You act as if you've never been visited by a dead person before," Mr. Free remarked with a chuckle.

"How... what... what are you do... huh," Bill clamored.

"I have come to help you get the company back on the right track Bill, it seems like we have come on some hard times."

Still staring in disbelief, Bill sat down in a chair across the room from Mr. Free, and he started talking to him as if he were a living person. "I don't know how I can see you, but I could definitely use the help you're offering." Bill sat for a moment collecting his thoughts. "Uncle Jack, I don't know what's going on. I've left all of your company policies in place but the numbers are worse than they ever were when you ran the company. Every day I try to figure out what went wrong, but I don't have a clue."

"Bill, there's not a problem with the company's policies; it's your perceptions," Mr. Free, explained leaning forward in his chair. "You are singularly responsible for what has happened to this company; it was all caused by your actions. Unfortunately, you don't possess the ability to see it."

Shocked that Mr. Free would blame the company's problems exclusively on him, Bill sat back in his chair and folded his arms.

"You are the cause of the problems at AceCalc, but I'll have to take some of the blame. You see, when I was alive I taught you how to work in my culture, but I ran out of days without teaching you how to lead the culture. You did the best you could with the tools you had, but your perceptions of effective management have been tarnished by the years you spent in traditional corporations.

Mr. Free picked up a pad of paper and handed it to Bill without saying a word.

"Bill, above everything else, you need to understand the following: To create a meaningful life experience for anyone requires one thing above all else, it requires life. Your organization is a living organism. Just like any other living organism it is healthiest when it breathes freely. Conversely, when it's having trouble breathing it shuts down. When I was leading AceCalc it was a breathing organization. Now it's a suffocating organization. For your organization to breathe again, you, as the leader, need to supply oxygen."

Bill had absolutely no idea what Mr. Free was talking about. He continued taking notes, but he was completely lost.

"Bill, I'm going to teach you about what I call 'The Six Business Suffocators.' Regardless of the quality of talent, systems, or past successes in an organization, if any of these six suffocators are allowed to creep into an organization they will act as an illness. These illnesses spread until the organization can no longer breathe. All six of these suffocators are plaguing AceCalc, today."

In order to lead any organization effectively, one must keep these suffocating perceptions from creeping into their culture. If a leader does not continuously put effort into keeping these suffocators out of their organization the suffocators will creep in and destroy the organization's culture. Although the

six suffocators I'm going to discuss with you are interrelated,
it is critical that you understand each one individually, in
order to expunge them from this organization quickly, and
keep them away in the future."

"Uncle Jack, I don't mean any disrespect, but I have several problems with what you're saying. First, I don't understand what you're talking about with all of this breathing stuff. Second, I really don't think I'm the reason this company has fallen into disrepair," Bill stated with a hint of anger in his voice.

··

"Look Bill! I don't have time for a lot of meandering discussion. AceCalc is in an emergency state and it needs to be fixed immediately. You're the only one who can turn this ship around. The faster I can teach you what you need to know, the faster you can start the repair process. I know you don't agree with everything that I'm saying right now, but I think that you will agree with me that AceCalc is currently broken?"

Bill nodded.

"Can we also agree that what you're currently doing to improve the situation at AceCalc is producing few results?" Mr. Free continued.

Unable to make eye contact with Mr. Free, Bill nodded again.

"Then can we work with the assumption that trying anything else will be better then continuing to do the same things that you've been doing up till now?"

After a moments hesitation Bill agreed. "Okay, Bill. Let's start by discussing the first suffocator. I want to begin by going back to a discussion you had with one of your former vice presidents."

The next thing Bill knew he was floating over two people in the conference room closest to Bill's office. He was watching a heated conversation between two people. The first person was Bill; the second was former Chief Financial Officer, Tracy Baldwin. After listening for a few minutes, Bill recognized the conversation that had occurred a few months ago. Bill and Mr. Free watched the dialogue unfold.

"Look Tracy, I guess you've forgotten this, but you actually work for me, and if you want to continue working for me you will never contradict me in a meeting again," Bill arrogantly opined.

"But… um… I was just stating my opinion in a meeting," Tracy replied, confused by Bill's tone.

"You obviously have an attitude problem, and I don't need anyone in MY organization who will act like this. I think it will be best if you consider this your termination!" Bill exclaimed.

After slowly getting out of her chair, Tracy walked toward the door of the conference room. Glancing back at Bill she noticed a look of superiority flash across his face.

After watching the episode, Mr. Free turned to Bill and asked him why he felt as if he had to act so arrogantly.

"Well, she challenged my opinion during a senior staff meeting. I told the senior staff that we were changing a part of the company benefit program and she voiced dissention in front of the entire group. That was the second time she had contradicted me; she should have known better," Bill said.

"But what's wrong with her voicing an opinion during a meeting? Mr. Free responded puzzled.

"She shouldn't challenge me in front of other employees. She works for me, and she has no right to act that way," Bill replied, as if Mr. Free should've already known this.

After the slightest smirk, Mr. Free blinked his eyes once and transported both of them to a bench behind the AceCalc building.

"I've seen many occurrences like the one we just observed over the past few months. This brings me to the first suffocator; I call it 'Misuse of Authority.'" Mr. Free and Bill stood and began walking around the pond, as they continued talking about the events they had just watched. "Bill, authority is a desire that stems from the ego. You are making a mistake that stems from a misperception of leadership that is currently way too prevalent in traditional corporate cultures. Too many managers think being IN CHARGE is important. They think that there is some kind of practical business purpose in having your employees think you are superior to them. Any time these managers feel as if someone in their organization is challenging their authority, they turn it into a battle. These battles are very damaging to an organization. You are, essentially, putting your own desire to feel important above every other employee's need to feel valued and appreciated in their jobs. You need to understand that authority is actually a battle for oxygen.

When you decide to exercise your authority over one of your employees you suffocate them. At this point, they are just going to go through the motions of working. They stop caring about the success of the organization, and instead, only concern themselves with their own survival. Simply stated, the moment you treat someone as if they work for you rather than an organization, they will immediately start working against you."

Bill struggled with this concept. The power games that he had seen in the corporations that he had worked for over the years were so deeply ingrained in him that he assumed they were somehow necessary for business to occur. "But Uncle Jack, the AceCalc employees actually do work for me. I run the company, so everyone in the company works for me," Bill replied as if Mr. Free's words were silly and trivial.

"Really? That's interesting." Mr. Free replied calmly.

Suddenly Bill found himself back in his office standing in the exact spot where he was when he first saw Mr. Free. He looked at his watch and realized that no time had gone by. After contemplating his conversation with Mr. Free for about twenty minutes, Bill went about his day as usual. He went through some emails and phone messages and then left his office to grab a muffin from the cafeteria.

Bill turned a corner and took a few steps into customer service before he realized that something was very wrong. Everyone in the department was gone. He ran into the delivery department and saw that everyone in that department was gone as well. After running in a circle around the first floor he realized that he was the only one in the building. Bill panicked. He didn't know what to do next. Dozens of phones were ringing, but no one was there. He ran out to the parking lot to see if anyone was still there. All of the cars were gone. He tried to page the vice presidents and received no response. Finally, he sat down and put his hands over his face.

Bill heard a voice say, "Do you want some pretzels?" He took his hands away from his face and realized that he was in an entirely different place. He was sitting at a back table of the local bar, The Free Zone with Mr. Free. He took a number of deep breaths, thinking through what had just occurred. "Relax Bill, it didn't really happen. It was a day dream."

After taking a moment to compose himself, Bill responded. "Why did you do that Uncle Jack?"

"I wanted you to better understand that no one in your organization really works FOR you. Every employee in this organization represents you. When they interact with a client they are your representative. Your role is to make sure that they are treated in a way that enables them to represent you in a productive manner during their dealings with clients and other employees. Remember what you learned in training about creating a meaningful life experience. Your short-sided misperception that the other employees work for you, blocks their ability to make their jobs meaningful to them at a human level. One of the keys to employees finding meaning in their jobs is the perception that they are an important contributor to the organization. They need to feel valued as people. When you treat them as if they are pawns, it blocks them from emotionally connecting to their work. This is what I mean when I talk about breathing. Your employees are not going to feel that they can take a deep breathe until they feel appreciated as equal contributors. Think about your own feelings Bill. How do you react when someone treats you like you are small and unimportant? Does that stir you to do your best?"

Bill thought about his own career and how he felt when his bosses had treated him like he was unimportant. He remembered how defensive he got. How he would spend the rest of the day complaining to other employees about how he was being treated. How he started doing as little work as possible when one of his bosses made him feel insignificant. For the first time he realized that the employees at AceCalc must be doing the same. He began to realize that there really wasn't a practical business purpose for using authority as a management tool. Before he could speak again Mr. Free continued.

"I have one more important point to make on this subject. I know you have not changed any of the policies. You guys have each potential employee go through a laborious interview and training process. The people AceCalc hires are very qualified."

"I think so."

"This is another reason why none of AceCalc's employees work FOR you, Bill. Any employee who is qualified to work in this organization could easily get a job somewhere else."

"I think that's true, Uncle Jack."

"If an employee could go across the street and get a job tomorrow then they are definitely not working FOR you; they are working for themselves through your organization. They will do this as long as they feel that it is personally rewarding for them to be here. That's why the meaningful life experience for employee's concept was originated. We wanted every employee to feel that their job was an integral part of the quality of their life. We wanted them to feel as if leaving AceCalc would be like leaving a significant part of their life behind. When you started treating them as subordinates it slowly dissolved their connection to the company.

One by one employees, like Tracy Baldwin, felt as if their jobs were no longer a meaningful part of their lives. Their hearts left AceCalc when they felt unappreciated, and soon after, their bodies left too. This is one of the biggest reasons why AceCalc currently has the highest employee turnover it has ever had. To turn this around you have to put an end to your self indulgent misperception that the people in this organization work FOR you.

Bill was starting to catch on. As they continued to walk around the pond, Bill and Mr. Free discussed situations from Bill's experiences with past employers. He was starting to see how much damage his former managers had done with their reliance on authority in interacting with employees. He had never really thought much about this practice. As their discussion continued, Bill started to laugh at himself a little; his misperceptions of the role of authority seemed rather silly. "I don't understand why I couldn't figure this one out on my own," Bill said with a chuckle.

"There are lots of irrational management practices. Your emotions were keeping you from seeing your actions from a healthy perspective," Mr. Free explained. As Bill and Mr. Free continued to talk the entire tone of their conversation became positive. "Let's talk about hierarchy, Bill. When you first came to AceCalc, you learned that we have no hierarchy. You didn't change this policy, but you acted as if there was a hierarchy, which is just as bad. Now that we've had this discussion, do you have a better understand of why this is a flat organization?"

"Well, I understand that there's no practical purpose in treating an employee as a subordinate. I guess this is the same idea on a grander scale. To get the most out of employees they have to feel appreciated and respected as equals."

"Good, I look at it this way, everyone at AceCalc is equally important to the organization's success. Everyone is playing a role in achieving one unified goal; creating a meaningful life experience for clients, employees, and owners. You are all working toward the same goal; thus, having a hierarchy serves no purpose. Your role as the CEO is not getting people to think that you are more important than they are, rather it is getting the most out of everyone in the organization. These two concepts contradict. You can only achieve one or the other; you can't achieve both."

"Let's look at another recent occurrence in the organization, Bill." In the blink of an eye, Bill and Mr. Free were hovering over the accounting department. Bill immediately recognized the event that they were watching. It had occurred about a month ago. AceCalc has a phone system that records every voicemail that is left with any employee in a backup queue. This system was originally put into place so that the company would have a record of phone calls in case they ever had a legal dispute. Thinking that his employees were dropping important business items, Bill decided to start listening to the voicemails on a daily basis. On this particular day, Bill had heard a voicemail that a client left for the accounting department...

"Hey guys, its Katie Brantley at Pioneer, I think you guys forgot to send us an invoice for the extra three items we ordered on the fourteenth. Give me a call when you get a chance. Thanks."

After hearing the voicemail from Pioneer, Bill sprang into action. He walked into the accounting office and told all of the employees to huddle around him. "Listen up everyone. I just heard a voicemail from Pioneer saying that we didn't invoice them for money that they owed. We can't afford to miss billing opportunities, so this is what we are going to do. Every time that a non- cycle billing occurs we're going to put it on this whiteboard with the date and the amount. This way we won't miss any of our extra billings. I went by the call center, and they gave me a list of twenty items customers purchased off-cycle in the last month. Here's the list; This is $2,900.00 worth of off-cycle purchases," Bill said, "We need to watch this stuff. We can not be this sloppy."

After Bill left the room, the Director of Accounting, Ashley Rynken, went through the items on the list that Bill had brought. After looking up each item in the computer she told the staff that each of them had already been billed. Additionally, the phone call that caused Bill to react was merely a minor misunderstanding. From above, Mr. Free and Bill watched a discussion between Ashley and one of her coworkers, "I hate it when he does that; anytime a minor deviation from the regular business process reaches his desk he thinks we have to reinvent the wheel. Then to make matters worse, he tells us how HE wants us to reinvent the wheel. It's very frustrating. He makes us feel like we're idiots."

"Bill, this situation is a perfect example of a bad habit you've developed. For some reason you think that you know better than your employees."

"What do you mean Uncle Jack?"

"When things get tough, or when anything out of the ordinary happens, you take authority away from your employees by telling them how things should be done. Every time you do this you cause two problems. First, you insult your employees' hard work and expertise. You have hired good employees. In this particular case, you have over 80 years of accounting experience in that department. When you tell them how to do things you trivialize their efforts. Those employees will not care about AceCalc as much in the future, due to your actions. Second, you turn all of your employees into drones; I call this 'creating a company brain drain'. You reduce the company down to a bunch of followers. This is a massive waste of talent. To achieve the level of success that AceCalc once had, you must have all of your employees mentally engaged in accomplishing the company's purpose."

"But Uncle Jack, I know the policy. I know that all brains matter."

"Yes, but that is just the beginning. You know that policy, but when you misuse authority and create a suffocating culture you block people from voicing their ideas. In this case, by telling them how they are going to do things in their own departments you are communicating that you think you know better than they do. Once you convey this message your employees stop focusing on the company purpose and instead focus on following your orders. A business never grows through usurping employee authority, which reminds me of something else I noticed the other day."

Next thing he knew, Bill was standing in front of the main suggestion box that was located in the downstairs central hallway. The box was a little beat up, the lock no longer worked, and the paper tray that always sat next to the box was empty.

"Bill, how is this beat up box promoting recommendations?"

"Um, uh, well"

"If you were an employee, would this dusty, old box motivate you to suggest ideas?" Mr. Free inquired.

Bill looked down at the ground contemplating his answer. Before he could reply, Mr. Free continued.

"Let's look at something else, Bill."

Mr. Free took Bill back to a moment Bill had shared with his assistant a few days ago. Bill's assistant handed him a recommendation that had been hand delivered by one of the team leaders in deliveries. Bill snatched the recommendation out of his assistance's hand, looked at it for a split second, and then trashed it. "It's amazing how stupid these people are!" Bill commented toward his assistant.

"Let me get this straight, Bill," said Mr. Free "Since you became CEO the company has fallen on the worst times it has ever seen, yet you feel that other people's ideas are stupid? Bill, do you remember how I used to hand-write thank you cards to every employee who submitted a suggestion?"

"Yes."

"Why did you exchange the hand-written notes for impersonal preprinted thank you cards?"

"Writing all of those cards seemed like a waste of time, Uncle Jack."

"Bill, this company was built through employee ideas. You should do everything possible to promote a flow of ideas throughout the organization. You should constantly reward and support what I call the 'effort of ideas'. That is, you should always act as though there are no bad ideas. Everyone who takes the time to offer their ideas should be rewarded without exception."

Before Bill could respond, Mr. Free had transported them again. They were now sitting in two wooden chairs in an empty room. Although he could tell that they were somewhere in the AceCalc building, Bill couldn't tell exactly where they were.

"Let's talk about breathing again. I want you to do an exercise with me. Sit up straight in your chair. Clear your head of all burdens. Picture yourself sitting on the warm sand of a perfect beach watching the sunrise. Everything is completely calm. You don't have a care in the world. Can you picture it?"

"Yes, very calming."

"Wonderful, now take a deep breath. Inhale as deep as you can and hold it for two seconds. Now, slowly exhale."

A smile came to Bill's face. He felt more relaxed than he had in many years.

"Now I want you to change one thing. This time, before you take the deep breath, picture how you felt when one of your old bosses treated you like an inferior subordinate instead of treating you like a valued and respected contributor."

Bill took a deep breath and then looked up at Mr. Free, "My breath felt restricted and short. It wasn't relaxing like the previous breath."

"Now, do the same exercise again with the 'brain drain' concept that we just discussed. How do your deep breathes feel when a boss throws out your ideas and tells you to do something his way, even though your way was working well?"

"That gave me a sickly feeling when I exhaled," Bill replied with a grimace.

"That's what I mean by 'A Breathing Organization'. You want all of your employees to feel that they can breathe comfortably everyday just like your first breath during this exercise. This is a very useful exercise. As we go through more of the suffocating concepts, don't just view them from a business perspective, do this exercise and see how your breathing is affected when you think about one of the suffocators. The way that the suffocators affect the depth and clarity of your breathing is exactly the same as the way it affects the organization."

Misuse Of Authority:

1. The moment you treat staff members like they work FOR you they will begin to work against you. No one worth having as an employee actually works for you. They work with you as long as it is beneficial for them to do so.

2. Do not put your personal desire to feel powerful over employees need to be respected and appreciated.

3. You do not know better than your employees.

4. To get exceptional results you must nurture and empower employees so they will bring their ideas to the table every day. Reward all contributions regardless what you think of their legitimacy.

5. Never treat anyone like a subordinate. It blocks them from putting meaningful effort into their jobs.

6. A fully functioning organization is a group of individuals breathing clearly, fully, and without restriction.

CHAPTER 7

The next morning Bill headed to work earlier than he had in many months. He felt invigorated. He couldn't wait to start using the lessons that Mr. Free had taught him the previous day. For the first time in as long as he could remember he felt as though he had control of what was occurring around him.

Just like the day before, Mr. Free was sitting at Bill's desk reading the morning paper when he arrived. "I've been waiting for you, Bill. After all, we ghosts don't really have to sleep," Mr. Free said with a chuckle.

"Uncle Jack, I feel really good about the stuff you taught me about authority, yesterday. It changed my entire perception of leading our organization."

"Great Bill, but you have a lot more to learn. Today we're going to discuss the second suffocator."

Bill rushed to sit down and take out his note pad. "Go ahead, Uncle Jack."

"There's actually something occurring as we speak that will illustrate this suffocator quite well" Mr. Free folded his newspaper, took a sip of his coffee, and with a smirk toward Bill and a blink of his eyes, he transported them both to a discussion between a director and an employee in the call center. The director's name was Derek Hass; he had recently been promoted to the position, and he had only been with the company for about two years. The employee he was speaking with was a veteran. Tracy Brookings had been working in the call center for about four years. She was very well respected; in fact, she'd never had a negative comment on an employee review until recently.

"Tracy, I've been looking at your numbers, and I don't think we're on the same page. Your call times have not improved at all," Derek asserted.

"Derek, we've discussed this before. I've been working with some of these clients since I first came to AceCalc. These clients are my friends. It goes without saying that I will spend a lot of time on the phone with them," Tracy replied with great frustration in her voice.

"But these numbers are a priority. Every call center employee has to keep their calls under two minutes," Derek replied.

Scooting up in her chair, Tracy quickly replied, "I've been working here for four years and all of a sudden people care about call times. I remember when people used to care about things that mattered like client retention and the company's purpose."

"Look Tracy, I'm going to lay it out straight for you. I'm getting a lot of pressure concerning these call times. I've been told that my department has to get under two minutes per call or else I could lose my job. This is now the focus from the top. I need you to address this issue because my manager will come down on me if I don't. Please help me out. I like you, but I need to keep my job."

Immediately after Derek uttered his last words, Bill and Mr. Free were transported back to Bill's office.

"Uncle Jack, I didn't tell anyone to ignore the company's purpose," Bill stated as if he was in trouble.

"No, you didn't, but you took away their ability to focus on the purpose. You have successfully confused all of your employees," Mr. Free replied.

"What do you mean Uncle Jack?"

"The second suffocator is inconsistency, Bill. You can completely suffocate your staff by sending them inconsistent messages. In the discussion that we just witnessed, Derek was completely blocked from focusing on the company's purpose because his manager gave him a focus that contradicted the purpose. He was told that he could lose his job if the call times did not decrease.

At this point all he could think about was what needed to be done to keep his job. This trickles down to every employee that he touches. The next thing you know, everyone is singularly focused on the call times."

"But why can't they focus on both the purpose and the call times?"

"They can focus on multiple items, but if you want this to happen, you have to get your managers to equally focus on several items. Generally this is very difficult. The items that receive the most attention from the top will become the employee focus. There is a cycle to this. A department will have a deficiency in one area that is important to upper management. Upper managers will tell lower managers that they have to get the specific area in line. The lower managers will tell all of their employees that they must focus on that one particular item. Next thing you know, all emails, employee praise, employee reprimands, and the greater part of the department's discussions are focused on this one item. As more focus is put on this one item, it takes away from many other areas of the business. As I stated before, employees are going to focus on the items that get the most attention. That's how a company's focus wanders away from what's truly important. I had a good friend who used to work for a rental car company. The office that he ran was one of the most profitable in the area. He was consistently recognized for his office's success. About a year into his job a new general manager came into the area. The new manager thought that charging clients for fuel was very important. The entire focus became fuel. It became more important than business growth, customer service, profitability, or employee issues. His manager would call him at 7:30 in the morning just to ask him how much fuel his office collected the previous day. The next thing you know, my friend was being written up for his lack of fuel charges. In one of the months during this period he had the most profitable office in the entire system and he was on probation because of fuel. It's a damaging cycle. A lot of managers think that you can focus on these little things and still maintain the more general company purpose. While it seems possible theoretically, in practice it's impossible".

"So how do we focus on little areas that need improvement?" Bill asked.

"First and foremost you have to tie them to the company's purpose. Second, you have to make sure that all recognition for adherence to the issue matches both the company's purpose as well as the focus of each employee's position."

"So what would you do with the call time issue, Uncle Jack?"

"I probably wouldn't make this an issue at all. It doesn't seem to match the company's purpose of creating a meaningful life experience for clients. The only reason call times should be an issue at AceCalc is if the hold time to get to a live person is too high and we feel we can't maintain our client's memorable experiences, and reduce hold times without adding employees. Let's look further into this issue. I would address this issue in the following manner. First, I would tell the call center staff that clients are waiting on hold too long. Then, I would ask them what they think should be done to reduce hold times, while maintaining the client's meaningful experience. If, as a team, the call center staff decides that hold times are a problem, then they should brainstorm ways to fix it as a group. The key is that any solution must be completely focused on maintaining the company's purpose. I've found that the best solutions to most business problems resolve the problem while maintaining all other factors."

"Now I understand that all company focuses should be aligned with the purpose or else the purpose becomes irrelevant," said Bill, "but I don't fully understand why you call this suffocator 'inconsistency?'"

"This example is only one part of it. There's a lot of truth in the statement you just made though. You said, 'if each focus does not match the purpose then the purpose becomes irrelevant'. This is completely true, but it's only the tip of the iceberg. Inconsistent communication voids all organizational structure. When managers confuse their employees by giving them inconsistent messages, they make the company's purpose irrelevant as well as making all of its systems irrelevant. In most cases, as inconsistency increases, any focus on the client gradually dissipates. This is not the path to great results, or even good results for that matter."

"So how do I get everyone in the organization to adhere to this concept?"

"You have to make consistency a management focus. You have to constantly be watching for this suffocator. It's so easy to let this one creep into a department unless you constantly teach your managers the importance of consistency. It's actually rather simple; give everyone in the organization a simple and consistent path to follow, and make sure that every company communication matches the company's purpose. Let's look at another way that inconsistency can suffocate a department."

With a blink of Mr. Free's eyes, Bill found himself hovering over a sub-department within the call center. This particular group of employees deals with new clients. This group consists of a manager (Kyle), two shift leaders, and fifteen employees. Bill and Mr. Free were observing a conversation among three long term employees.

"I can't believe that Stacy got the promotion to shift leader. Her numbers were worse than all of ours."

"Yeah, it doesn't make any sense. I've heard rumors that it only happened because she's dating the manager."

"I don't know if that's true, but it's complete favoritism. He just picked the person who sucks up the most."

"That person is going to be me next time. It's obvious, now that kissing Kyle's ass is the way to get a promotion."

Bill and Mr. Free viewed this discussion for a few more minutes and then Mr. Free transported Bill back to his office.

"I don't think that manager actually promoted Stacy because they were dating. These three employees are wrong," Bill insisted.

"That doesn't matter, Bill. If the employees perceive that the promotion was unfair, and no one makes an effort to address it then the rules change. From this point forward those employees are going to focus on catering to what they perceive the manager cares about rather than focusing on the company's purpose. This manager created a culture completely focused on himself, just by being making decisions that were inconsistent with company policies. Even if you're right, and he didn't promote based on bias; he broke the company communication policy."

"What do you mean Uncle Jack?"

"One of the employees we just observed submitted a request to discuss the issue with his manager and it was ignored. As you know, its company policy to address all employee concerns and never leave any issue gray. By not being consistent with this policy, the manager has completely shifted these employees' focus from the clients to himself. I always looked at it this way; employees must feel that they are on solid footing in their jobs if they are going to have a meaningful life experience at work. When employees don't understand what's expected of them, they aren't on solid footing. If employees are left unclear about their objectives due to inconsistent messages, it suffocates their desire to perform to their best abilities. They must feel that they are on solid footing with a clear path to success." Mr. Free stopped to give Bill time to finish writing down notes. After a minute or two he continued. "Bill, picture yourself walking in the rain. You take a step and you slip and start to fall. What do you do next?"

"I try to stop myself from falling so that I don't get hurt," Bill replied.

"Exactly, your focus goes from whatever you were doing to your personal survival. You are forced to think only of yourself. In a business situation, when an employee feels that she's on unstable ground, she can only focus on her own survival. That's how suffocation works; breathing requires consistency. Inconsistency destroys company cultures."

Just as Mr. Free finished talking he disappeared, and Bill found himself sitting in his office alone. As he had come to expect, no time had gone by. Bill looked through his notes and highlighted the following concepts.

Inconsistency

1. All communication must be simple and consistent.

2. All company recognition and focus must match the company's purpose.

3. Give your staff a path to follow and do not give them any reason to think they need to divert from that path in order to be successful.

4. Focus on consistency throughout all departments and managers. Make sure everyone understands the importance of consistency to the business' success.

5. Understand that even the smallest inconsistency can cause a damaging ripple effect in the company's culture. These inconsistencies must be addressed, immediately.

CHAPTER 8

Later that afternoon, Bill was already putting his new found knowledge to work. He was talking to one of the vice presidents about the importance of conveying a consistent message when talking to the staff in his departments. Mid-sentence, Bill was lifted out of the room and transported to his office by Mr. Free.

"Did you see, Uncle Jack? I was talking about the inconsistency issue."

"That's great, but you have another issue to address before you can address inconsistency," Mr. Free replied.

"Is it so important that you had to pull me out of a meeting?"

"Yes. Without this understanding, the rest of these lessons are worthless. Besides, you've already learned that no time goes by when I show up so what are you worried about? When you get back everything will be just as though you never left," Mr. Free stated with a chuckle.

Bill nodded.

"I wanted to talk to you about your morning announcements."

"I still do them just like you did, Uncle Jack."

"I like your morning announcements, Bill," Mr. Free said with a warm smile. "Let's listen to the announcements from this morning."

Mr. Free moved them to an area of the building from which they could observe two delivery department employees listening to the morning announcements. Bill watched as the two employees laughed and made sarcastic remarks during his announcements. After Bill made an announcement about a position opening up in accounting, one of the employees that were observing turned to the other and said sarcastically, "Isn't this the third time that position has been available this year?" Later in the announcements, after Bill made a comment about an improvement to the employee benefits program, after which one of the employees said, "I'm sure Bill will just cut a benefit somewhere else to make up for that," and they both started laughing.

After the last announcement concluded, Mr. Free transported the two back to Bill's office to discuss what they had just observed.

"I guess we have a few employees who need to go, huh?" Bill stated as if what they had observed wasn't a big deal.

"Actually, Bill, I've observed comments like this throughout the company on a daily basis. You'd have to fire more than half the staff."

"So what's the problem, Uncle Jack? You told me that you like the way I do the announcements."

"The problem isn't the announcements; it's the employees' opinion of the person making the announcements."

Bill was taken aback by Mr. Free's assertion. "What does their opinion of me have to do with the announcements?" Bill asked.

"Bill, this is an example of the next suffocator. Your words are irrelevant because there's no trust in the organization anymore."

"Why would that be? I haven't lied to anyone."

"A number of things are occurring to create this scenario."

"So what's the fix?" Bill asked as if he was addressing a minor annoyance.

"First, I need you to understand why it's occurring. Before I do though, let's go to the pub, I'm a little thirsty."

Mr. Free blinked his eyes and transported them to a booth at the pub. Although Bill was fully aware that other people couldn't see the two of them, he was still amused by the fact that people could pass right through them.

"The biggest thing I want you to understand is that without trust there's no leadership. Distrust decays the organization in a way that no other mistake can. This goes beyond simply trying to be an honest person. You have to make sure that trust is at the root of every company policy. If you don't actively focus on trust, the company rumor mill will gradually suck the trust right out of the organization. It doesn't take much to cause doubt."

"So how do I address this?"

"You have to understand that there are actually two intertwining concepts that make up this suffocator. Employees trusting you, and you trusting them."

"What does trusting the staff have to do with anything?"

"I guess that's a good place to start. Employees will act according to the way you treat them. If your communication shows that you don't trust them, then most employees will find reasons to make it so. If your communication shows that you do trust them, then most will live up to that trust. You're treating your employees like they're criminals."

"I don't understand... how am I doing that?"

"Well, let's take a look at a few issues that have come up. About six months ago you thought you could save some money by cracking down on the use of account 2421. You thought that employees were stealing from the company by using this account. The entire time I ran the company, monies employees "wrote off" to this account was approximately $8000 per month. You decided that you could reduce this amount by making employees fill out a form describing why they were using the account each time they used it. After six months you had successfully reduced the use of 2421 by about 20%. At the same time, the total company losses attributed to theft have almost tripled. What did you actually accomplish, Bill?"

"I still don't understand the connection, Uncle Jack?"

"When you put policies in place that, at their core, assume dishonesty, you treat your employees as criminals. When you make them feel like criminals it decays the trust within the organization. Many employees will respond to this treatment by proving you right. They will look for ways to steal. This is a damaging cycle. The more policies you create that teach employees that you don't trust them, the more they will act in accordance with your actions."

"So how do I handle my issues with employee theft?"

"You have to improve your communication concerning how employee theft affects the overall success of the entire company, thus affecting the success of each individual employee. Teach the staff that each theft, regardless of how minor, affects bonuses, salaries, and other areas of the business that are important to them."

"Employees won't respond to that," Bill replied sharply.

"They won't right now, but in the past, when the company was actually creating a meaningful life experience for employees; they would have cared about the role of theft on the company's success.

Right now none of your employees believe that they are in control of their futures with AceCalc. They have no trust in the systems or the promises that their managers are making. At their core, these are all trust issues in one form or another. If you want to decrease theft you, first, need to reinstate the trust within the organization. One of the keys to accomplishing this is avoiding policies that communicate a lack of trust."

"But what if they continue to steal?" Bill asked.

"If you still have an issue with theft then you have the wrong people. Those who steal even when their job is fulfilling all of their emotional, psychological, and financial needs are few and far between. Most of them will be low performing employees who get weeded out based on performance. The vast majority of thefts that occur in organizations can be directly attributed to the way employees are treated. Companies always try to fix the problem by adding policies and firing the offenders. More often than not, the problems are within in the company's culture not the individual employee."

After a few more minutes of discussing trust based policies, Mr. Free moved on to his next issue. "Bill, let's go look at another area of the AceCalc building." Mr. Free transported them to a busy hallway in the middle of one of the call centers. "Bill, do you know when the last time you stood here was?"

Bill thought for a second and then responded, "How am I supposed to know that, Uncle Jack? I walk around the building all the time."

"Actually Bill, you don't. It's been over a year since the last time you stood in this spot."

"So what does that have to do with trust?" Bill replied sarcastically.

"Everything! No one trusts people they don't know. For some reason you've stopped talking to front end employees. Most of these employees only know you by name. How do you expect them to trust you when they have no idea who you are? To them you are just an empty suit. Since you make no effort to interact with them, they believe anything that they hear about you though the rumor mill."

Mr. Free was right. He had stopped getting to know front end employees, but until recently he hadn't really understood why. It all had to do with authority and power. Until Mr. Free taught him how detrimental his reliance on power had been to the organization, he went out of his way to make sure that everyone in the organization knew he was THE BOSS. This focus had caused him to create a distance between himself and from front end employees. He thought that if employees knew more about who he was, it would cause him to look weak in their eyes; and if he looked weak, it would usurp his authority. Until recently, he saw this as a major management mistake. "Uncle Jack, we don't have to discuss why I haven't been interacting with front end employees. I understand my error. What should I do to make things better in this area?"

"One of the biggest keys to building trust is showing people your true self. They have to feel like they know your heart. You are expecting them to make their jobs at AceCalc a meaningful part of their lives. Let them know why you work here. Let them know why AceCalc is a meaningful part of your life. Before employees will trust you, they need to see you as a human being instead of an empty suit. You need to make an effort to get involved with their lives. I used to spend almost every weekend with an employee's family. I would go to family picnics, children's sporting events, charity functions, and anything else an employee would invite me to. I loved it."

As had become the norm, after Mr. Free made his final point he transported Bill back to the exact place from which he had taken him. The vice president he had been talking with was staring at Bill wondering why he had stopped talking mid-sentence. Bill took a moment to regain his composure. Recalling what he had been saying before Mr. Free had transported him, Bill began speaking again. After he finished his discussion with the vice president, Bill headed back to his office anxious to summarize his notes from the day's discussion with Mr. Free.

The Keys to Preserving Trust

1. You teach employees how to act. If you treat them like criminals they will fulfill your expectations. Eliminate any policy that exists only to address the assumption of dishonesty.

2. We only trust human beings. Before employees can trust you. They must feel that they know who you are. Communicate your feelings and show that you are interested in your employee's lives.

3. If they don't trust you, they won't care about their jobs; if they do not care, they will not produce meaningful results.

4. Without trust nothing else matters. As a leader you can't assume trust. You must take steps to actively promote and preserve trust.

CHAPTER 9

Buzz... buzz... buzz... buzz.

Bill slapped his alarm clock and headed toward the kitchen to get some breakfast. He turned his radio on to NPR for background noise while waiting for his waffles to pop out of the toaster. While listening to the news he made snide remarks to himself about the stories he was hearing. After listening to a senior economic advisor discuss economic issues he growled, "Idiots, I can't believe these people are considered experts." As the words left his mouth, Mr. Free appeared on his couch.

"Hi, Uncle Jack, just getting ready to go to the office."

"I see."

"So, what brings you to my house this morning?" Bill asked.

"Something you just did reminded me of one of the suffocators that I need you to learn."

Thinking through his day up to this point, Bill couldn't figure out what he possibly could have done that was linked to the business in some way, "What did I do Uncle Jack?"

"When you were listening to NPR a moment ago you seemed to have something negative to say about half the people who spoke,"

"So what?" Bill replied while looking for his car keys.

"You do this at AceCalc too. You think that you know better than everyone else in the organization. You've completely stopped listening and you have no respect for anyone else's opinion."

"Uncle Jack, didn't we talk about this during the discussion on misuse of authority. I think I get it; opinions matter," Bill remarked, thinking that Mr. Free had already forgotten that they had discussed the issue.

"Bill, this isn't a discussion about valuing opinions as it relates to authority. This is much more elementary. Before, we discussed how you were downplaying the opinions of others because you wanted everyone to respect your authority as their boss. You thought that by acknowledging the intelligence of your employees, you would lose your stature as the person 'in charge'. You now understand that the opinions of your employees are valuable, and that reliance on authority has little to do with business success. However, you have a more basic problem; you simply don't listen to people."

"What are you talking about? I have ears! How can I not be listening?" Bill replied as if Mr. Free's insinuation was silly.

"Let's look at something that happened just yesterday."

Mr. Free blinked and transported them to the scene of a conversation between Bill and the head of the accounting department.

"Bill, I have some ideas on how to decrease overdue receivables on senior client accounts, but an old policy that is still on the books is blocking me from making the changes I need to make," the accountant stated, while she and Bill walked quickly down the hall,

"We need to leverage some new technologies that were not available when the policy was written..."

Bill interrupted her, "Thank you for your input; I will consider your idea. Right now I have to get going."

"But, I just need... "

Bill walked off, waving to the accountant as he headed out the front door of the building.

Back at Bill's house, Mr. Free continued with his lesson. "You completely blew off her concern, Bill. You treated her opinion like it was completely irrelevant."

"But Uncle Jack, I'm very busy. I don't have time to listen to everyone who wants a minute with me."

"Um... so let me get this straight Bill. The company is in terrible shape, and you don't have time to listen to people with ideas. I don't know what's causing you to be so busy, but it doesn't seem like it has much of a positive effect on the company's results," Mr. Free asserted, just to show Bill how short-sided his previous 'I'm too busy' comment was.

After looking at the ground for a moment and twiddling his thumbs, Bill realized that he had been using the 'too busy' excuse a lot in order to get out of tense situations. As Bill shifted uncomfortably in his seat, Mr. Free continued with his lesson.

"Bill, employee ideas have driven this company forward since its inception. You need to treat everyone's ideas like gold. Some of them might be coal, but in order to get the good ones, you have to value the bad ones as well," Mr. Free stated with a dismissive chuckle. He blinked his eyes again and transported the two of them to a nearby park. The two men walked through a playground while discussing the issue further. "The suffocator I want to discuss today is called 'false communication'. When I ran AceCalc, the flow of communication throughout the organization was highly effective. Since I've been gone the 'true communication' has dwindled."

"What do you mean, Uncle Jack?"

"There's is a vast difference between mere talking and actually communicating at a level that benefits the organization. To get the most out of your staff's talents, you must create an organization in which the staff feels empowered to express the opinions necessary to promote the company's purpose. You've created the opposite."

Bill was confused. He didn't understand how his actions were limiting the ability of employees to effectively communicate. He didn't even see how he could significantly affect the organization's communication flow. Even though he didn't understand, he had learned over the past few days that he had to keep an open mind about the lessons that Mr. Free had to teach him.

"The first key to creating a culture of true communication is becoming a good listener. As the leader, you actually affect listening throughout the organization."

"What are you talking about Uncle Jack? How in the world can I control the listening?"

"When you disregard your employees' opinions, you teach everyone in the organization that they are allowed to disregard the opinions of others. This trickles through every department. You are the leader; anything you do in front of an employee teaches. Good communication starts with good listening. You really need to genuinely listen to every single opinion that's offered. You have to be an active listener. Ask questions. Understand the idea, the problem that led to the idea being presented, and the thought process behind the idea. This is the key to turning ideas into company improvements. This is also the key to creating true communication within the organization."

Bill was speechless. He knew he was guilty of poor listening. As they walked, he thought about all of the times that he had ignored an employee's opinion since he had become CEO. He had turned it into a habit. As soon as someone started presenting an idea, he'd put up a wall.

"The problems you cause by leading this way are twofold. While the loss of good ideas is relevant, it's not the greater issue. The greater damage is what you communicate to employees when you ignore their ideas. When you teach employees that their ideas are unimportant, you create a disconnect between them and the organization. All of a sudden they feel that their importance to the organization and their ability to contribute to its success has decreased. This disconnect is very damaging. It affects an employee's attachment to their job and, in turn, the effort that they put into their job on a daily basis. All because you taught them that their opinion doesn't matter."

"So how do I fix this, Uncle Jack?"

"First, you have to actively communicate the importance of every opinion. You must reward every attempt to contribute to the organization. Every idea has to be given the same consideration as your own. Second, you have to give regular feedback. I liked to send the contributor an email telling them that I had received the idea, as well as who would be taking the next step with their idea. Later, I would follow up on the idea. I made sure that the contributor knew exactly what happened with their idea. Regardless of whether it was adopted or not, they were thanked for their contribution, and I made sure that they understood why their idea was or was not adopted. If you communicate with the staff in this manner, they will feel like valued contributors. Let's revisit a situation that I witnessed a few months ago."

Mr. Free blinked his eyes and transported the two men to the scene of a call center employee complaining about one of his orders getting lost in the deliveries department. "This is the third time that Cheryl in deliveries has messed up my client's order. She's mistyping the size dynamics on the Smith Construction orders. I don't know what else I can do to address this. I've called her three times, and I've called her manager to request a meeting, I've mentioned it to our manager, but no one will address this issue. I might lose this client if this continues."

The second that the employee finished his statement Mr. Free transported Bill back to his house.

"That was a quick one, Uncle Jack."

"That's all you needed to see, Bill. Why do you think that problem is continuing to occur?"

"Apparently a couple of my managers aren't doing their jobs."

"Yes, but that's not the heart of the issue. It goes deeper than merely not addressing the problem at hand. Why aren't they doing their jobs Bill?"

"I don't know, they're busy and they don't see this as a priority?"

"They aren't addressing this issue because of the culture that you've created. They're completely focused on their own needs and it's blocking all communication. They repel any issue that appears to be the fault of their department rather than addressing it. Back when I was here, people were focused on the company's purpose above all else. In a situation like this, the four people involved would get together and, without regard to fault, find a solution that best met the company's purpose. Now, all people do is point fingers; opinions are seen as attacks rather than opportunities to improve. Staff members are more concerned about looking good to their bosses than resolving issues. As suffocators crept into the organization, each employee put continuously greater focus on their own survival. In this case a suffocator has completely blocked true communication between departments, from occurring. In order to communicate on a meaningful level, staff members have to be able to breathe."

Bill began putting this together in his mind with what he had already learned about inconsistency, misuse of authority, and trust. He saw AceCalc's communication problems as one of the many by-products of the suffocators he had already learned about. "I think I get it, Uncle Jack. AceCalc's employees have become too inwardly focused as a result of the issues we've been discussing over the past few days. As they began to shift their focus onto themselves, they stopped all dialogue that could potentially damage their employment status."

"Yes, you're starting to get it. By the way, I have a term for the scenario we're discussing. I call it 'survival mentality'. Survival mentality occurs when suffocators in an organization block breathing and cause employees to focus exclusively on their own survival to the detriment of company's purpose. Let me give you another example, I noticed the picture of you helping Habitat for Humanity build a house for a needy family last summer."

"Yeah."

"Helping Habitat is definitely an outward focused cause. You're helping another family improve their lot in life, but let's suppose that, in the middle of painting a wall, you start to feel short of breathe. After a few seconds it gets progressively worse. After a few minute you collapse. You're doing everything you can to get the smallest amount of oxygen to go through your lungs."

Visually shaken by the mental picture, Bill put his hand on his chest while continuing to listen to Mr. Free. "That's terrible, Uncle Jack."

Ignoring Bill's comment, Mr. Free continued his story. "Notice what's happened here. At the point that your ability to breathe decreased, your focus changed from helping others build a house to getting yourself enough air to survive. Your focus instantly shifted into survival mode. That's why I call it 'survival mentality'. It's exactly what happens when suffocators limit an organization's ability to breathe."

Mr. Free's example really put things in perspective for Bill. Although he'd learned a lot up to this point, he now felt it more personally than he ever had before. For the first time he understood how his poor leadership had affected his employees. Overwhelmed, Bill asked Mr. Free if they could continue their discussion on communication later. Bill needed some time to absorb everything that he had learned that day. Mr. Free agreed and disappeared.

....

The next morning Bill was walking away from his weekly executive staff meeting when he looked to his left and saw Mr. Free walking right next to him.

"Morning, Uncle Jack. Why am I being visited right now?"

"Bill, I want to talk to you about the meeting you just had."

"I'm pretty happy about the way the meeting went, Uncle Jack. I used a lot of the stuff that you and I have been talking about."

"Yes you did, Bill. You're doing a great job of letting go of the perceptions that have been ingrained in you and accepting new ideas. I'm proud of you."

A big smile came over Bill's face as Mr. Free complimented Bill's efforts.

"I want to talk to you about two more items that have to do with true communication, because a suffocator crept up in your last meeting."

Bill thought about the meeting, hoping he could figure it out without Mr. Free having to tell him. After a few moments he replied, "It seemed like a good meeting to me. What happened?"

"Nothing happened; that's the problem. Nothing meaningful happened at all."

"What do you mean, Uncle Jack?"

"You've turned your staff, and in turn, your entire organization into a bunch of 'yes' men and woman. No one feels like they can be honest anymore."

"I know, I know, I've misused authority and all that other stuff, and now my staff is suffocating."

"I appreciate the fact that you understand these important concepts, but there's more to it than that. I've seen this suffocator creep up even in relatively healthy organizations. As with all of the other suffocators if you don't actively address this one, it will find its way into your organization. You have to promote open dialogue; you can't just that hope it's occurring."

"How did this suffocator creep into the company?"

"This suffocator is caused by a number of different leadership mistakes. Your biggest mistake is the way you treat honest communication."

"What do you mean?"

"Let's look at your executive staff meetings. Through your actions you've created a detrimental unofficial policy that I call 'the hush'. The hush is very easy to create. All you have to do is communicate to the staff that you don't react well to bad news."

"How did I do that, Uncle Jack?"

"I'll give you an example. Last week, your CFO voiced some concerns about the P/E account balance. Not only did you dismiss his concerns during the meeting, but you didn't talk to him for an entire week. You put him in your dog house. You've done this many times to people who have voiced bad news."

"So I need to start handling bad news better; is that the fix?"

"That's a good start, but the problem is much more complex. When you started having a negative reaction to bad news, all of your managers started doing the same thing. This has been going on for so long that all of your employees have been taught that honesty doesn't help their careers at AceCalc. Now everyone just agrees with everything that trickles down from you through management."

"Can I fix this, Uncle Jack?"

"Yes, this is fixable. There are two major keys to fixing this issue. First, reread your notes about creating a culture of trust. In order to bring honest communication back into the company, you must bring back the trust. Second, you must develop and implement a strategy that will turn AceCalc's culture into a company culture that promotes sticking your neck out. No one should ever be reprimanded for offering honest feedback. Any negative reaction to honesty, either officially or unofficially, is very damaging to your effort to promote honesty. Once everyone understands that there won't be any negative repercussions for speaking their mind, you will have to promote the benefits of what I call 'active honesty'. You must create heroes. Anyone who offers honest feedback that correlates with the company's purpose should be heavily praised for sticking their neck out. The more you promote their efforts, the more other employees will see the benefits of being actively honest."

"So I need employees to understand that giving honest feedback will benefit their careers?"

"Exactly, but you're still underplaying it. You want your staff to understand that there's a direct correlation between active honesty and major rewards. Understanding that these actions will benefit their career is helpful, but active honesty is so important that it requires a much higher focus. Employees need to see that honest feedback is so valued that it can turn any employee into a company celebrity."

Bill sat for a few moments trying to absorb what they had just discussed. "This is going to take some effort."

"Active honesty is rather difficult to implement, but the reward is worth the effort. Most companies don't put enough effort into this area of leadership. Since it's not a direct problem, they don't give it enough attention. Those who do embrace this concept and actively pursue its implementation reach a level of effectiveness that most business leaders can't even conceive. Keep in mind that honesty is the anti-politic, and it must be sought passionately every day. You either embrace it or you don't, there's no halfway."

Back in his office, Bill took a long sip of his soft drink, slowly leaned back in his chair, and looked down at his notes on true communication. Anxious to put his new knowledge to work, Bill asked, "So is that all I need to learn about communication? I feel like I have a ton of work to do to fix all of this?" Bill asked.

"There is one more thing. This one is simple though."

Bill flipped to the next page in his notebook and said, "Let me have it."

"Simply stated, as a leader you are constantly communicating regardless of the actions that you take. You cannot not communicate. Everything you say, as well as everything you don't say, creates an effect. Additionally, it's impossible to over-communicate. Every change that occurs in an organization must be addressed. Don't ever assume that people know about everything that's going on in the organization. When you make this assumption, you allow silly gossip to suffocate productivity. For example, I was just reading this email from one of the directors in the deliveries department," said Mr. Free, pointing to the open letter on Bill's computer screen.

Bill,

Several of my team members have asked me if AceCalc is going to be sold to an investment company. Can you address this rumor, please?

David Kirshe

"Are you planning on addressing this concern, Bill?"

"Why should I address such silly rumors, Uncle Jack?"

"The reason that that particular rumor is going around is because you gave a tour of the facility to a group of guys last week.

You should've addressed this visit in your morning announcements. Since you didn't, the rumor mill has addressed it for you. I call this suffocator 'under-communication,' and it's just as dangerous as inaccurate communication. When staff members hear a message repeatedly, it doesn't really do any damage, but when staff members don't hear a message at all, it does a great deal of damage. It doesn't matter if a few people hear something important repeated ten times, as long as everyone who needs to hear the message does, in fact hear the message. It's very easy to under-broadcast a message, but, for all practical purposes, it's almost impossible to over-broadcast it."

As had become the norm, Mr. Free disappeared moments after finishing his last sentence. After rushing to a meeting, Bill took some time to look over his notes and summarize his thoughts on true communication.

False Versus True Communication

1. The first key to communication is listening. Really listen to what's being said. You'll be amazed at what you will learn.

2. Staff must be able to communicate between departments in order to produce the results that best match the company's purpose. Expunge the 'blame culture'; It creates friction and blocks productivity.

3.   Promote open dialogue. Don't let an informal 'hush policy' enter the culture. Those who have the courage to be messengers of bad news should be respected. Don't kill the messenger.

4.   You can not not communicate. As the leader everything you say and everything you don't say makes waves throughout the organization. Many leaders badly under-communicate.

5.   You can not over communicate. Important concepts should be broadcast constantly. Don't ever assume that everyone has heard the message. This is almost never the case.

CHAPTER 10

The next time Bill saw Mr. Free there were no pleasantries. Bill was working at his desk when he was instantly transported to the sales department where he observed a weekly sales meeting led by the newly promoted sales director, Kyle Cessler.

"I'm going to make this very clear!" Kyle blared at his sales staff. "If each of you doesn't start selling the insurance upgrade at least 60% of the time, I will have to document it as non-compliance, and it will affect your paychecks."

After listening to Kyle's rant for a few minutes, Mr. Free transported Bill back to his office for a discussion.

"So Bill, what do you think about Kyle's management style?"

"He is very direct, but sometimes you have to be that way, Uncle Jack."

Leaning back in his seat, Mr. Free folded his arms and took a deep breath before talking again. "Bill, the next suffocator I need to teach you is more of a general understanding that's at the core of many other suffocators that we've discussed. It's important to understand this concept individually if you want to keep it out of the organization."

"What is this suffocator? Uncle Jack?"

"Let's use the meeting that we just observed as an example. Why was that manager yelling at his staff?"

"He was trying to motivate them?" Bill answered, wondering if he was missing something. "Yes Bill, but what tactic was he using to motivate them?"

After thinking about Kyle's meeting, Bill replied, "I guess he wanted his staff to think that if they didn't perform they would lose something that's valuable to them."

"What emotional reaction was Kyle attempting to get from his staff?"

Bill thought for a moment, "He wanted them to be afraid of losing something, right?"

"Yes Bill; fear is the suffocator. In business as well as in life, fear destroys productivity, creativity, and human potential."

"But Uncle Jack, Kyle's sales team is producing meaningful results," Bill asserted.

"How are you defining those results?"

"The sales numbers are well above average."

"That's true, but you're not looking at the entire picture."

"What do you mean, Uncle Jack?" Bill asked while shuffling through some papers looking for his most recent sales reports.

"Sure, Kyle is producing adequate numbers but his employee turnover is among the highest of any department in the company. Think about how much it is costing the company to constantly train new sales people because of his management style. Additionally, consider how many sales people who could have been assets to the company for years to come, have left the company because of Kyle's suffocating management style. The price of fear management does not always show up on spreadsheets. Much of the damage is intangible."

Bill pulled out a calculator to get a clear picture of the amount of money they were losing do to the high turnover in Kyle's department. After making a few calculations he shook his head as he realized that these costs reduced the actual profit from the department to almost nothing.

"Since we are focused on this particular sales department, let's look ahead for a moment. You will recall Kyle threatening disciplinary action if his staff did not sell the insurance upgrade to each client. Let's see what affect this actually had on his staff."

Mr. Free blinked his eyes and moved Bill to a conversation between two of Kyle's staff members. The conversation they were observing had occurred two weeks after Kyle had made the threat in the meeting. The two staff members, Rich and Brian, were both above average performers. Since making the threat in the meeting, Kyle had 'written up' two employees for not having improved their insurance upgrade sales.

"Rich, how are your upgrade sales going?"

"I had a good day in the field today, but I did not sell any upgrades," Rich replied while preparing his sales sheets before submitting them to Kyle.

"So what are you going to do? Tracy was 'written up' last week for her lack of upgrade sales and she had the best number of all of us for the week."

"I am going to manipulate my sales sheets so it looks like I sold the insurance upgrade. If I make it look like I gave the client a discount on shipping, I can move that money over to the insurance line and it will look like I sold the insurance."

"That's a good idea, Rich. I am going to start doing that too," Brian replied while making himself a note to modify his future sales sheets.

After watching the conversation, Mr. Free blinked his eyes and moved the two to a nearby barber shop.

"Uncle Jack, why are we at the barber shop? Am I going to learn something here?"

"No, I just wanted to stop by and see how Joe is doing. He cut my hair for over 25 years." The two sat in the corner and discussed the conversation they had just watched between the sales team members.

"So Bill, what do you think of the conversation we just watched between Brian and Rich?"

"I don't know Uncle Jack; it seems that they are not doing what is best for the company."

"That's true, how would you handle this situation Bill?"

"I would pull them aside and let them know that their dishonesty on the sales sheets will not be tolerated," Bill replied confidently.

"That is how most companies would handle an issue like this one. Handling it in this way represents a complete misunderstanding of breathing."

Bill's expression completely changed. He leaned back in his chair and continued listening.

"The problem is not with the employees. They are merely reacting to the culture around them. Their manager put them in a place in which they felt they had no other option but to manipulate the system. This is what happens when fear enters the culture. These staff members have been forced to focus on their own survival which blocks them from focusing on the company purpose. This is a miserable situation to be in for an employee."

"I see. They are so afraid of losing their job, or some other negative repercussions from their boss, that they are unable to focus on anything else," Bill replied while thinking through the issue.

"This is the role that fear has in suffocating an organization. Additionally, don't lose focus on the company purpose. You saw the behavior fear created with Rich and Brian in the sales team."

"Yes."

"What does any of this have to do with the company purpose? These employees are so afraid of their boss that they are manipulating numbers. What does that have to do with creating a meaningful experience for these employees? Additionally, creating a meaningful experience for clients has been completely forgotten in the scenario we watched in the Kyle's department."

Without a moment to contemplate the concepts that they had just discussed, Mr. Free moved Bill to another conversation. This time he was watching a long time delivery driver named Sachin talking with one of the clients. Sachin had been a delivery driver for over ten years. He was talking to a Beverly Morissette at the Morgan Advertising Agency. Sachin had known Beverly for over five years.

"Sachin, I need a few items outside of our normal order. I know I did not put these items into my order, but I did not know I needed them when I called you guys on Monday."

"What do you need Beverly?"

"Do you have any D2489 process disks?" Sachin looked down for a second to think about the request. The disks that she was requesting came out of the 'select' inventory. In the past he would have been able to go straight to the inventory management staff and get as many disks as he needed for the client. Lately, however, they had not been willing to give employees disks without a processed purchase in the computer from a member of the call center. One of Sachin's coworkers had recently gotten a monumental run around attempting to pull inventory without a processed purchase.

"Beverly, I would like to help you but I can't. I can no longer pull same day inventory. Can you call it into the call center? I will get it to you by Friday if you call it in now."

"I don't understand Sachin, we have always been able to do this in the past," Beverly replied.

"Beverly, you know me very well and you know that I would do anything I could to help you guys out... you just need to understand that AceCalc is not the same place it was when Mr. Free was alive. I just can't afford to get in trouble. I have two kids to take care of and I need this job. I am really sorry," Sachin replied obviously frustrated.

After talking for a few more minutes, Sachin slowly walked back to his truck. After sitting in the driver's seat and putting the key in the ignition, he sat back in the seat and daydreamed about the way things used to be. He felt completely powerless. He thought about the effort he had put into his job over the years. He thought about providing for his family. He worried about the future. He no longer believed that doing a good job necessarily meant that he had job security. Things had changed so much. Every day he feared that some random occurrence would leave him without the job he had committed his life to.

With a blink of his eyes Mr. Free moved Bill to a park a few miles away from the AceCalc building. Walking through the outfield of a little league baseball park, neither Mr. Free not Bill said anything for several minutes. Bill was obviously strongly impacted by the events he had just observed. The message that Bill was supposed to learn by watching Sachin was crystal clear. He could not have seen a more impactful example of fear destroying his organization.

"You see Bill, fear affect so ma..."

"Uncle Jack, if it is alright with you, I need some time to think about what we just observed. Can we continue this talk later?" Bill asked, interrupting Mr. Free in mid-sentence.

Seeing that Bill was consumed by the events they he had just witnessed, Mr. Free patted him on the back and then disappeared. Bill found himself back at his desk by himself. After a few minutes thinking about what he had learned about fear, Bill decided to take a walk around the AceCalc building. As he walked, he noticed so many things that had previously not reached his consciousness. Walking from department to department watching staff members work, he realized that fear had permeated every area of the business. All of the positive energy that was the life of AceCalc when his uncle was alive, had been suffocated away. He saw no smiles, no laughing, and no life. The passion that employees used to have for their jobs and for the company was gone. Thinking about his uncle's breathing references, he could see how he was leading an organization that was struggling for air. He now had a clearer understanding of how bad things were at AceCalc. While he thought he understood before, seeing Sachin tied him in more emotionally than ever before.

As had become his habit, Bill headed home for the day to go over his notes. After looking over his notes from the day for quite some time, he then wrote down his daily summary:

A Suffocating Fear

1. Fear is not an effective motivational tool. The damage fear based motivational methods has on an organization far outweighs the benefits.

2. Fear focuses staff to focus on their own survival at the expense of company and individual objectives.

3. Fear kills all staff risk taking. There are no cultural heroes in a culture suffocated by fear. Everyone is so worried about their own survival that they will not consider sticking their neck out.

4. Fear suffocates all positive human energy. All passion, excitement, enthusiasm, and positivity are sapped away by fear.

CHAPTER 11

Thinking that he was in bed, Bill rolled over to see how much time he had until his alarm went off. As he turned over, he realized that he was actually sitting on the thirteenth green at a local golf course with Mr. Free.

"Hi, Uncle Jack. What's going on?" Bill asked as he yawned and stretched.

Pointing at a near by oak tree, Mr. Free stated, "I wanted you to see something here at the golf course. Take a look at that tree."

"What am I supposed to be looking for Uncle Jack? It just looks like a tree with a bunch of birds in it."

"Take a look at that bird struggling on the ground."

Bill looked closely at a bird under the tree. It seemed to be caught in some sort of string on the ground under the tree. Uncle Jack! It looks like that bird is caught in a string. I hope someone comes along and frees it."

"Yeah, the bird can't fly while its wings tangled up in the string."

"I feel sorry for the bird," Bill injected, "but why are we here, Uncle Jack?"

"I'm using the bird as a symbol of suffocation. That bird is meant to fly. It's in his DNA to open his wings and fly freely. The string, in this case, is blocking the bird from its path in life. The same is true for your employees. When placed in a work environment that empowers and rewards them for bringing their passions, talents, and abilities to work everyday—using them fearlessly—your employees then will rise to the challenge, just as that bird will spread its wings and fly when its wings are not restricted. The six suffocating concepts we are discussing hurt your employees exactly as that string hurts that bird. It blocks the bird's ability to act in the way it is intended too."

"Is this the last suffocator, Uncle Jack?"

"Yes, in a way, Bill. The last suffocator is actually a summation of a few concepts that come from the same leadership misperception; I call this suffocator 'inward focus'."

Mr. Free blinked his eyes and transported Bill back to his house. Bill found his notepad and took a seat on the couch. Mr. Free made himself some tea and leaned on the kitchen counter.

"So what am I supposed to learn from the bird metaphor, Uncle Jack?"

"There are two lessons to be learned from the bird metaphor. First, it illustrates the damage that suffocators can cause in an organization. Each suffocator affects employee performance similarly to how that string affected the bird. Second, this is a lesson in perception..."

"Perception of what?"

"I went into HR the other day and looked at employee compensation numbers," explained Mr. Free.

"What's wrong with the employee compensation numbers? I have been able to reduce employee compensation expenses by 4% over the past 12 months," Bill stated confidently.

"That's the problem, Bill. Your perception of employees has changed. You once saw employees as a valuable part of our company's purpose. By using employee compensation as a way to reduce expenses you've proved that you no longer treat employees as the central asset of the business. Instead, you treat them as expenses just like the copy machine."

"But I do value employee contribution Uncle Jack," Bill replied not fully understanding Mr. Free's claim.

"No, you give it lip service, your actions don't match your words. As soon as you decided to nickel and dime that account, you started treating employees as if they were an expense that needed to be managed. But I don't want you to focus on the budget portion of this issue right now. Instead, I want you to focus on your perceptions of employees and why that led to treating employee compensation as an expense."

"What do you mean, Uncle Jack?"

"When I ran AceCalc our employee compensation was as high as it could be. We used an equation based on company profits. I always wanted to give employees as many rewards as I possibly could. We would calculate our profit, subtract all of our expenses, and then see how much money we had left over to put towards employee compensation. It was one of the many things I loved about running AceCalc. You have the exact opposite state of mind. You try to pay your employees as little as you possibly can, all the time. You treat employee compensation as a business expense; it's not a business expense. In order for something to be an expense there has to be zero benefit in increasing the money spent on it. For example, spending more money on electricity wouldn't help us in our efforts to achieve our company purpose. On the other hand, treating employee compensation as a part of our key to maximizing the meaningful life experience for employees, instead of treating it as a company expense, directly affects the company's success in achieving our purpose."

"So you're saying that I shouldn't worry about the budget, Uncle Jack?"

"You should only worry about the budget as it relates to expenses that have no effect on achieving the company's purpose. This actually brings me to another misconception. You have forgotten why we are here in the first place."

"I know why we are here. AceCalc creates a meaningful life experience for clients, employees, and management."

"Exactly Bill, so why are we talking about budget issues anyway? Profit numbers aren't AceCalc's main objective; they are a by-product of the company's purpose. When the company achieves its purpose, it will gain more profit than you could possibly imagine. If you want to have a more profitable company, increase your focus on the company's purpose and your profits will come. You've done the opposite. You're focused on the by-product rather than the purpose. I never paid much attention to the profit numbers. My job was achieving the company's purpose. The same is true for you."

Bill could see that even though he had been an AceCalc employee for many years, his perceptions and actions were still guided by the lessons that had been ingrained in him while working for more traditional companies. As soon as things started going bad at AceCalc, he lost focus on the company's purpose and went straight to the spreadsheets. As he worked to find ways to tighten expenses, he was essentially attempting to shrink the company into success. The more he lost focus on AceCalc's historically successful purpose, the worse things had gotten.

"There's a more general perception at work here that goes against your goals as the leader," Mr. Free continued, while pacing back and forth in Bill's kitchen. "You can't bring yourself up while holding others down. AceCalc's staff is the key to achieving the company's purpose, but when you nickel and dime them on compensation, you teach them that they are nothing more than tools for your success. It does not work this way. As we have discussed before, people act as you teach them to act. When you teach them that they are nothing more than tools to make you more successful, it suffocates them. That is why I call this suffocator 'inward focus'. As the leader, anything that you do strictly for your benefit will ultimately work against you. Leaders must be outward thinkers. They only succeed through the success of others. It's impossible for them to succeed while others in their organization are not. This is what I mean by 'you can't bring yourself up while holding others down.'"

Mr. Free's words completely changed Bill's perception of what mattered most at AceCalc. For the first time he was starting to understand what was truly going to be necessary in order to turn the company around. He'd spent so much time focused on the numbers that he had lost track of the company's true purpose and the people who were at the core of AceCalc's past success. He remembered something he'd been told by Mr. Free many years earlier that he hadn't thought of in a long time; "At AceCalc, all boats rise together. We succeed together, or we fail together."

Bill was excited about the lessons he was learning from his Uncle. Anxiously he asked, "So what else do I need to learn about 'inward focus' items, Uncle Jack?"

Mr. Free sat back in his chair for a moment and looked around Bill's office. Noticing all of the charts, graphs, and piles of paper that covered every inch of Bill's desk, he turned to Bill and asked, "What's your purpose every day when you come to work here at AceCalc?"

"I promote the company's purpose just like everyone else," Bill replied without hesitation.

"No, I mean as the leader, what's your primary purpose?"

"I'm not sure what you want me to say, Uncle Jack. What do you mean?"

"Every day you come to work and attempt to create a meaningful life experience for the people around you, correct?"

"Yes."

"As the leader, what do YOU do to make that happen?"

After a few moments of silence Mr. Free smiled. "It's alright Bill, I didn't expect you to know. I just wanted you to focus on the question. I believe that the single most important attribute of leadership is understanding how leaders become successful. This understanding is at the center of the inward focus suffocator."

"What do you mean, Uncle Jack?"

"Leaders can ultimately be successful by attributing one general perception to all of their efforts. They must focus all of their efforts on helping others become successful. It's that simple."

Bill wrote notes furiously while Mr. Free continued to talk, "To achieve the level of results that every leader dreams of, you must give up all inwardly focused concerns. All fears, personal insecurities, and selfish desires have to be ignored in order to truly lead. You can only succeed through the success of others. Every day that you come to work, your goal should be helping as many people as possible satisfy their wants and needs. This includes emotional, spiritual, psychological, and financial needs. The more impact you have in helping others satisfy their wants and needs, the more successful you will be as the leader. If those around you, including employees, clients, stakeholders, family and friends are able to satisfy there wants and needs, you will become more successful as the leader, and the more the company with thrive as a result. This is the key to truly affective leadership. There are no shortcuts. You must fully embrace this understanding if you want to lead AceCalc in a meaningful way."

Bill sat for a while thinking about what Mr. Free had just said. He thought about all of the mistakes he had made since becoming the CEO of AceCalc. The more he thought about these things, the more he realized how often he had been guilty of inward focus. He had made so many decisions based on his personal needs, without thinking about the overall effect that his selfish decisions would have on the company. He closed his eyes and took several deep breaths. As the air went in and out of his body, he could feel a calm coming over him that he had never felt throughout his adult life. When he shifted his focus away from himself and placed it on others, he could feel his fears melting away. All of the thoughts that used to consume him were releasing their grip. With his eyes still closed, Bill suddenly felt the room become extremely hot. He opened his eyes and discovered that Mr. Free had transported them to a new location.

"Where are we, Uncle Jack?"

"Oh, we're in hell," Mr. Free responded nonchalantly, as if this was a common occurrence.

From where they were standing, they could see a dinner table that was 50 feet long and three feet wide. Two dozen people sat at the table- 12 people on each side. The table was full of meats, fruits, vegetables, and deserts. Although there was enough food to feed a group twice the size of the one at the table, the people were starving.

"Uncle Jack, why are these people starving. There is food right in front of them."

"Look closer and you'll see."

Bill looked closer and noticed that each person at the table had a fork unlike any he had ever seen. The forks were three feet long. The people at the table would put some food at the end of their fork and try to turn the fork so that they could get the food to their mouths. However, because the forks were so long, they couldn't get any of the food to their mouths and remained starving. Everyone was extremely thin, they barely spoke, and they were all sad. They looked like they had been starving for months. The fact that the food was right in front of them was completely irrelevant because they didn't understand how to feed themselves. "They can't eat the food because the forks are too long. That is an awful trick," Bill commented.

"Is it a trick… let's see," Mr. Free replied with a calm smile.

In a flash Mr. Free had transported them again.

"Where are we now, Uncle Jack?"

"This is heaven," Mr. Free replied.

Once again, they were observing a long dinner table with the same dimensions as the one in hell. There were 24 people, just as before, with more food in front of them than they could possibly eat. However, unlike the group in hell, this group was enjoying the huge feast. They were eating as much as they wanted and enjoying each other's company.

"Does this group have different forks, Uncle Jack?"

"No, they have three foot forks, as well."

"Then how are they able to eat?"

"Look closer, Bill."

Bill looked closer and discovered the difference between this group and the group in hell. Even though they had three foot forks, the people in heaven weren't trying to feed themselves.

Instead, they each put food at the end of their own forks and fed the food to the person sitting directly across from them at the table. As a result, they were all able to enjoy the wonderful feast that they had been given.

"This is a wonderful example of the damage created by inward focus, Uncle Jack."

"Thanks Bill. So, are you ready to stop trying to feed yourself? Are you ready to start finding ways to feed your staff, clients, and stakeholders now that you know that this is the true path to leadership success?"

Bill smiled and said, "Yes, for the first time I am truly ready to lead AceCalc. Really ready."

Mr. Free patted Bill on the back and said, "I think so, too."

The next thing Bill knew, he was at home by himself. His notebook was sitting right next to him. With an energy and giddiness that he hadn't felt since he was a kid, he went through his notes.

Inward Focus and Leadership

1. As the leader, you can't bring yourself up while holding others down.

2. Employees are not an expense. You will only succeed when they succeed.

3. As the leader, your primary purpose is to help everyone around you achieve success in work and in life. The more you help others succeed, the more success you will achieve. There is no other path to successful leadership.

4. All selfish thoughts weaken your ability to lead. Let go of your inward focused concerns, fears, and wants in order to become an effective leader.

After going through his notes, Bill created the following sign to put up in his office and throughout the building.

These are the 6 organizational suffocators. If I allow one or all of them to creep into the organization these forces will suffocate all productive effort. Look for these destructive forces every day and snuff them out immediately if they manage to creep in.

- Misuse of Authority
- Inconsistency
- Mistrust
- False Communication
- Fear
- Inward Focus

CHAPTER 12

At 6:45 the next morning, Bill was already at the office. Reviewing some notes for the senior staff meeting he had scheduled the night before. Bill hadn't slept the night before. He spent most of the night going through all of the notes that he had taken during his time with Mr. Free. He had also spent considerable time thinking through what he was going to have to do to turn AceCalc around.

Although he hadn't had any sleep, Bill was wide awake for the 8:00am meeting. His assistant knocked on the door to his inner office to let him know that all of the meeting's participants had arrived. Moments later, Bill stormed into the board room. He had an energy and vigor that the group had not seen in years. Before getting started he took the time to walk around the table and shake everyone's hand. Then, he took a seat. The body language in the room represented years of Bill barking orders and otherwise talking down to the group. The two extra seats that were to Bill's immediate right and left were vacant. No one dared get that close to him. The group sat waiting for Bill to go around the room blaming all of the company's problems on them, as had become the norm. Bill waited a few moments for the chatter to die down and then began to speak. "Team, I am the reason that AceCalc is in the horrible situation in which it currently sits. All of the blame should start and end with me."

The group was stunned. Everyone's body language changed. They looked around the room to watch each others reactions. Bill pulled out a piece of paper on which he had jotted down a few notes and proceeded. "Guys, I'm turning over a new leaf. I've been doing a lot of soul searching, and I now have a better understanding of what made this organization so wonderful back when Mr. Free was here. I think it's time for us to get back to that place. I've made a lot of mistakes, and now that I know better I'm going to do everything in my power to do better. I'm going to change, and it's going to start right now."

Bill then turned to the company COO who was sitting to his right and said, "Brian, I am going to make you and everyone else a promise. I am going to ask you a question and you have my word that your answer will bring absolutely no negative repercussions toward you. I really want to know what each of you think. I am ready to start listening."

Brian smiled, sat up in his chair, and waited for Bill's questions. "First, in your opinion, what are the three most important changes that need to occur in order to improve operations?" Bill asked.

Brian thought for a moment and then stated his opinion. At first, he was very cautious because this was a side of Bill that they had never seen. However, as the meeting went on, Bill continued to show a desire for open dialogue by actively listening to all contributors. He even joked around a little, which he was not known to do. Gradually, the group became more comfortable with voicing their ideas, opinions, and concerns, so much so that the meeting lasted for several hours.

There was energy in the room that hadn't been felt in the AceCalc senior offices for a long time. The entire group left with a new-found optimism.

Although he had a lot of work to do, Bill left the office after the meeting and went over to the beach for a little while. He wanted to collect his thoughts before diving into the rest of his work.

After walking on the beach for about ten minutes, Bill decided to sit on an empty lifeguard stand. After pulling himself up the ladder, he leaned back and watched the waves. A smile spread across his face as he watched life go by in front of him. He was at ease with himself and more optimistic about the future than he had been in quite some time. He felt no stress. The worries that had plagued him for years had fallen away. He was breathing... really breathing.

Before becoming the CEO of The National Quilt Museum, Frank Bennett was a consultant, writer, and lecturer helping organizations nationwide with management and client development concerns. As a consultant, Frank has worked with a  diverse group of clients over the years including for-profit, nonprofit, and government organizations. Frank has spoken and conducted workshops at over one hundred organizations including Harvard University and Microsoft.

Frank lives in Paducah, Kentucky.

59403681R00096

Made in the USA
Charleston, SC
03 August 2016